C0-AKZ-680

International Federation of Library Associations and Institutions
Fédération Internationale des Associations de Bibliothécaires et des Bibliothèques
Internationaler Verband der bibliothekarischen Vereine und Institutionen
Международная Федерация Библиотечных Ассоциаций и Учреждений

IFLA Publications 29

Guide to the Availability of Theses

II Non-University Institutions

Compiled for the
Section of University Libraries and
other General Research Libraries

By G. G. Allen and K. Deubert

K·G·Saur München · New York · London · Paris 1984

IFLA Publications
edited by Willem R. H. Koops

Recommended catalog entry:

Guide to the availability of theses /
II, Non-University Institutions /
compiled by G. G. Allen and K. Deubert. –
München; NewYork etc.: K. G. Saur, 1984. –
VI, 124 p.; 21 cm. –
    (IFLA Publications; 29)
    ISBN 3-598-20394-2

Z 5053
A2 B67
1981
Suppl.
C. 2

CIP-Kurztitelaufnahme der Deutschen Bibliothek

Guide to the availability of theses / [Internat. Fed. of Library Assoc. and Inst.].
Compiled for the Sect. of Univ. Libraries and
other General Research Libraries. –
München ; New York ; London ; Paris :
Saur

2. Non university institutions / by G. G.
Allen and K. Deubert. – 1984.
    (IFLA publications ; 29)
    ISBN 3-598-20394-2

NE: Allen, G. G. [Hrsg.] ; International
Federation of Library Associations and
Institutions: IFLA publications

ISSN 0344-6891 (IFLA publications)

© 1984 by International Federation of Library Associations and Institutions
The Hage, The Netherlands
Printed and bound in the Federal Republic of Germany
for K. G. Saur Verlag KG, München
by Hain-Druck GmbH, Meisenheim/Glan
by Thomas Buchbinderei, Augsburg

All rights reserved. No part of this publication may be reproduced,
stored in a retrieval system or transmitted in any form or by any means,
electronic mechanical, photocopying, recording, or otherwise,
without permission in writing from the publisher.

ISBN 3-598-20394-2

CONTENTS

PREFACE

The need for a supplement to the Guide to the Availability of Theses
(IFLA Publication 17) so soon after the second edition compiled by
D.H. Borchardt and J.D. Thawley and published in 1981 was first
discussed in the Standing Committee of the Section of University
Libraries and other General Research Libraries at the Manila meeting
of IFLA in 1980. Attention was drawn to the fact that the Guide then in
the advanced stages of preparation was restricted to university theses
while, in many parts of the world there were numerous institutions of
higher learning, not formally designated universities, but which
nevertheless granted higher degrees by thesis. While there was some
doubt in the Standing Committee as to the actual extent to which
these other institutions were responsible for the production of theses,
it was agreed that the matter merited further investigation.

During 1981 the principal compiler of this supplement conferred with
D.H. Borchardt, and then carried out a pilot survey of non-university
institutions of higher education in nine countries across the world.
From 110 questionnaires that were distributed, 47 were returned. An
analysis of the responses was made and reported to the next meeting
of the Standing Committee of the Section of University Libraries in
Leipzig in August 1981. The Committee accepted the results of the
pilot survey as evidence of the existence of a substantial number of
non-university institutions of higher education from which
considerable numbers of theses, at both the masters and doctoral
levels, were emerging. It was agreed to submit a formal proposal and
request for financial support for the compilation of a further Guide to
the Availability of Theses from these non-university institutions.
Approval to proceed with the project was received in May 1982, and
subsequently a grant was appropriated to meet some of the costs.

The compilers of this present volume have relied extensively on the
work of D.H. Borchardt. His observations on the relevance of theses
to both the UBC and UAP programmes of IFLA are endorsed, and his
comments on national or institutional practices and on terminology
apply equally to the present compilation.

However, the compilation of this volume did raise some additional
difficulties. The 1981 Guide is restricted to theses presented to
universities, and although a small number of institutions that do not
call themselves universities was also included, these have mostly
established credentials of university standing despite this minor
distinction. The type example is clearly the Massachusetts Institute of
Technology, and such institutions are commonly to be found listed
among the formally designated universities in the widely available
directories of higher education. Non-university institutions generally
are much less adequately covered in the directories. For many
countries there are few, if any, entries, and for most the detail
supplied is limited and rarely indicates fields or levels of study
provided. Considerable work was therefore required to supplement
the information obtained from the major directories.

A second problem that emerged progressively as the project proceeded was that of the terminology in the names of the institutions. Whereas the concept of a university is readily identifiable in the names of those institutions in many of the languages of the world, the same cannot be said for other types of institution of higher education, or for all institutions in a minority of languages.

It has become evident to the compilers that the distinction between universities and other, non-university, institutions of higher education, cannot usefully be made on the basis of nomenclature. Thus in Finnish there are two terms "Korkeakoulu" and "Yliopisto" both commonly translated into English as "University", although the former might equally be considered to mean "Institute of Technology". Furthermore such terms as "Ecole supérieure", "Technische Hochschule", "Colegio", Politechnika", and many others carry a variety of meanings not immediately apparent to the native English speaker. Moreover, in the process of collecting information from these variously described institutions, it was revealed that some of them were, or had recently become, in reality integral parts of universities, and some had even changed their names to be known henceforth as universities.

Although the majority of institutions represented in this compilation are reasonably described as "non-universities', the compilers have been persuaded that the distinction is arbitrary and of little practical value for the purpose of determining either the availability of theses or even of assessing the possible merits of the work that these theses report. At an early stage in the project the suggestion had been made that institutions should be selected for inclusion on some basis of merit. Apart from the virtual impossibility of obtaining comparable assessments of institutions across the world, it has seemed to the compilers that to make such a judgment would be professionally inappropriate for librarians. It is the province of academic librarians to identify, describe and supply documents, but not in any formal way to advise for or against any particular documents. The compilers have therefore made no judgments but have presented such information as has been received from responding libraries.

Although the collection of data for this volume commenced immediately after the publication of the 1981 Guide, for a number of reasons, including those indicated above, returns from some universities not represented in the 1981 edition were received. It has seemed sensible to make this additional information available, and therefore to reflect both this formal change in the original perception, and the recognition of the impossibility of achieving a clear distinction between universities and other types of institution of higher education, in the title of this compilation. In designating it a "supplement" to the Guide to the Availability of Theses, the compilers envisage that a future edition will combine entries for all types of institution of higher education in the one work.

The Survey

Following the pilot survey conducted in 1981, the questionnaire was further modified, and in particular a question was designed to elicit information about the subject range of theses submitted to institutions. This was prompted by the realisation that many of the institutions are of a specialist character, or offer higher courses involving the presentation of theses in only a limited number of subject areas. The information gathered has been used to compile a subject index.

A mailing list of 1090 institutions in 50 countries was compiled from a variety of sources, the principal of which were :

ABC's of study in Japan, 1982-83. Tokyo, Association of International Education [1982].

Awards of the Council's Degrees of Master and Doctor of Philosophy. (Annual lists of theses). London, Council for National Academic Awards, 1969-1981.

College blue book. 17th ed. New York, Macmillan, 1979.

Directory of Japanese Colleges and Universities, 1979-80. Tokyo, Saikon Publishing Co., 1979.

Elenco generale delle università e facoltà ecclesiastiche (compresi gli Istituti "incorporati" e "aggregati"), (Vatican City), Holy See, n.d.

Les établissements d'enseignement supérieur et leurs formations. Paris, Ministère de l'Education Nationale, Direction Générale des Enseignements Supérieurs et de la Recherche, 1982.

International handbook of universities and other institutions of higher education. 8th edition. Paris, International Association of Universities, 1981.

La recherche a l'université : diplômes de 3e cycle. Paris, Ministère de l'Education Nationale, Direction Générale des Enseignements Supérieurs et de la Recherche, 1982.

World of learning, 1982-83. London, Europa Publications, 1982.

Stassen, Manfred (ed.). *Higher education and research student handbook.* Strasbourg, Council of Europe, 1980.

During 1982 and 1983 the questionnaire was distributed in English, French or Spanish as appropriate to the institution. In addition a Russian version was prepared, but, knowing of the difficulties experienced by our predecessors, we decided not to mail directly to institutions in the USSR. Instead, assistance was solicited from Russian colleagues active in IFLA. It is with regret that it must be reported that despite several promises of support, and the forwarding of the Russian version of the questionnaire, no returns were in fact received from that country. Subsequently, an account of the situation regarding theses in the USSR was noted in the Library of Congress Information Bulletin and, with the permission of the author, this is reproduced below.

3

Despite the mailing of a reminder letter, and 70 replacement copies of the questionnaire, the final response was a rather disappointing 248. Moreover, from these returns only 199 actual entries in the guide could be compiled. The discrepancy between the responses and the number of entries is explained variously. Some libraries reported that their institutions did not offer awards by thesis; some gave so little information that it has not been possible to construct useful entries; some responding libraries proved to have been included in the previous Guide; and one library sent in two replies at different times. Nevertheless this represents a significant addition to the 698 institutions recorded in the 1981 Guide, and certainly justifies the decision of the Section of University and other General Research Libraries to support the project. It should perhaps be noted that out of the 1090 institutions identified as possible repositories for theses, 432 were in the USA from where only 125 replies were received. The response rate was also particularly disappointing from Eastern European countries with the notable exception of Poland, and from Latin America. Some difficulties were experienced identifying institutions or addresses, in France and Japan in particular, and the considerable later distribution of questionnaires to those countries may have limited the response achieved.

Arrangement of the Guide

The arrangement and organisation of entries in the 1981 Guide was studied and discussed extensively with colleagues practising in reference services. Unlike universities, the institutions responding to our survey are not generally identified by a name including a geographical element. It therefore seemed inappropriate to impose a place name on the filing element. In this supplement entries are arranged alphabetically by the official name of the institution within countries. The official name is that used in the country concerned, transliterated where necessary. An English version of the name is given in parenthesis where this has been considered useful.

To facilitate identification of particular institutions indexes of the names of institutions and of the geographic place names where they are located, are provided. There is also an index of institutions by subjects in which they have reported awards by thesis.

The format of presentation of the content of entries has been varied from that of the 1981 Guide, and an effort made to make the entries more self-explanatory. Each entry is identified by a running number, which is used for reference from the indexes, and the official name of the institution. This is followed by the title of a position or office that has been nominated as the permanent contact point. Where respondents provided only a personal name this has not been recorded. The preliminary part of the entry concludes with the name and postal address of the library.

The major part of each entry is organised into six sections, identified by roman numerals, thus :

I Awards
   The title of each award is given, followed by the numbers of

theses successfully presented in each of the years 1979, 1980 and 1981, in parenthesis, e.g. M.A. (20,25,31).

Notes indicate if more than one copy of a thesis is deposited in the library, if the library selects only some theses, or if the thesis is but a minor or optional component of an award.

II Publishing information

III Library access
Access through consultation in the library, by personal and/or by inter-library loan, is indicated.

IV Copying, purchase and exchange provisions
Many respondents indicated that they impose no restrictions on the photocopying of theses. However, as most countries have copyright legislation which in some cases applies to theses, we have used the phrase "no special restrictions on copying" to indicate the most common situation.

V Bibliographic control
The availability of information about theses in library catalogues, national or other bibliographies, or an institution's own publications, is provided.

VI Other information
In this section other libraries, institutions or organisations which hold copies of theses are recorded.

In the 1981 Guide a number of useful general comments were made on the situation regarding theses in specific countries. For the most part no additional information of this kind has been received and therefore it has seemed unnecessary to repeat these statements. In a few cases some general comments have been provided at the head of each national group of entries where some new information had come to our attention.

Acknowledgements

The compilation of this supplementary Guide has, like the 1981 edition, depended upon the efforts and support of many individuals. The initial encouragement and continuing support of members of the Standing Committee of the Section of University Libraries and other General Research Libraries of IFLA, and particularly that of Messrs D.H. Borchardt and A.J. Loveday who have been the chairmen through the years of this project, made the work possible. A grant of 4,250 Dutch florins from IFLA has met the costs of the questionnaire and its distribution, and of the final typesetting. Special mention must also be made of the assistance of Mr Sozo Nakano, National Diet Library, Japan, and the Sacra Congregatio pro Institutione Catholica of the Holy See, for their assistance in identifying appropriate institutions to be included in the distribution of the questionnaires.

From the staff of the library of the Western Australian Institute of Technology, has come the expertise and effort to prepare and conduct the survey, compile the entries and to prepare the typescript. Particular appreciation is due to Mrs Vicky Anderson who undertook most of the work of the pilot survey and the initial design of the questionnaire, to Mrs Sonia Babaeff, Mrs Dorota Podgorska and Mr Andre Mali who translated the questionnaire into Spanish, Russian and French respectively, to my co-compiler Ms Katherine Deubert who carried the major burden of the compilation of entries from the questionnaire and the construction of the indexes, and to Mrs Mary Matthews who undertook the keyboarding of the manuscript into the Library's word processor.

With the compilation of this project the Section of University Libraries and other General Research Libraries may feel some satisfaction for a job that it is hoped has been well done. However, it is a job that, in the nature of bibliographical compilation, is never complete and never finished. If this, and the earlier Guide, are to remain useful they will, sooner or later, need revision and extension. Those who use this Guide would encourage the present and future compilers, and the Section of University Libraries and other General Research Libraries, if they would communicate their comments, commendations or criticism of this publication to us or the Chairman of the Section.

G.G. ALLEN
Western Australian Institute of Technology
South Bentley, W.A. 6102, Australia

A note on theses for higher degrees in the U.S.S.R. by Robert V. Allen:-

A Soviet scholar is awarded a graduate degree, that of "kandidat" or of "doktor," after a process that includes a public defense of a thesis. As a means of informing the examining board and others concerned of the contents of each thesis, an abstract (in Russian, "avtoreferat") is published. These abstracts are customarily printed in an edition of only some 200 copies, however, and are not ordinarily made available for distribution outside the degree institution and some of the Soviet libraries of record. Although it may happen that these dissertations form the basis for articles or books, this is not always the case, so that the abstracts at times may be the only printed record of the research that has been done. Because Soviet doctoral degrees are customarily granted to senior scholars who may already have a considerable background in research and publication, and because abstracts at the doctoral level generally provide a bibliography of scholar's previous writings, these materials may be of considerable research value.

Heretofore, the Library of Congress has acquired only scattered examples of such abstracts. It is apparently still not possible to acquire a full range of such materials. Following some success over the past years, however, the Library has recently acquired from the Lenin State Library microfilm of some 80 dissertation abstracts on the history, culture, economy, and political life of the United States. Among topics treated are the concepts and methodologies of historians Arthur M. Schlesinger, Jr., Richard Hofstadter, and Louis Hartz, the suffragist movement, U.S. Bangladesh relations, the muckrakers, the outlook and methods of *Time,* American studies of Soviet history, and congressional influence on foreign policy in the 1970s. Other recent acquisitions of such abstracts have concentrated on themes from American literary history.

Both because of their value for bibliographic information and because of the illustrations they provide of the breadth of Soviet scholarly interest in the United States, these microfilms will be useful to Library patrons. These films are currently being processed for addition to the resources of the Microform Reading Room.

(Reprinted from *Library of Congress Information Bulletin,* v.42(30): 237-8, 1983).

AUSTRALIA

001 CANBERRA COLLEGE OF ADVANCED EDUCATION

Associate Librarian (Readers Services)
Library
PO Box 1, Belconnen, A.C.T. 2616

I   Master's (18,29,27).
    Each subject area has its own course work/thesis requirements.

II Not published.

III No restrictions on Library access.
    Available on inter-library loan within Australia and abroad.

IV Copyright is held by the author.
    Copyright law applies.
    Not available for purchase or exchange.

V   Listed in the Library's catalogue.
    Indexed in *Australian education index.*

VI -

002 CHISHOLM INSTITUTE OF TECHNOLOGY

Academic Services Librarian
Caulfield Library
PO Box 197, Caulfield East, Victoria 3145

I   Master's (2,2,0); Postgraduate diploma (15,20,14).
    Both are undertaken by course work plus thesis.
    Also offers Postgraduate diplomas by course work alone.

II Not published.

III Available for 2-hour Library use only.
    Not available for personal loan or inter-library loan.

IV Copyright is held by the author.
    Onus is on the author to ensure compliance with copyright law.
    Not available for purchase or exchange.

V   Listed in the Library's catalogue.

VI -

003 CUMBERLAND COLLEGE OF HEALTH SCIENCES

Head
Resource Centre
PO Box 170, Lidcombe, New South Wales 2141

I   Master's (1 in 1982); Postgraduate diploma.
    Both are undertaken by course work plus

thesis/research project.
Theses/projects are held by the School concerned and one copy is deposited in the Resource Centre.

II Not published.

III Library access is at the discretion of the Head of the Resource Centre.

IV Copyright is held by the author.
User is required to sign a copyright declaration.
Copying at the discretion of the Head, Resource Centre and author (if necessary).
Schools may be willing to exchange but would seek author's permission.

V Listed in the Library's catalogue.

VI -

004   MELBOURNE COLLEGE OF ADVANCED EDUCATION. CARLTON CAMPUS

Chief Librarian
Education Resource Centre
757 Swanston Street, Carlton, Victoria 3053

I Master's (3 in 1982).
Undertaken by course work and/or research project.

II Not published.

III Library consultation under supervision.
Not available for personal loan.
Original is available for inter-library loan within Australia and abroad.

IV Copyright is held by the author.
Copyright law applies.
Not available for purchase or exchange.

V Listed in the Library's catalogue.

VI -

005   NEW SOUTH WALES INSTITUTE OF TECHNOLOGY

Information Resources Service
PO Box 123, Broadway, New South Wales 2001

I Master's (5,6,9).
Undertaken by thesis or coursework. Also offers Postgraduate diplomas by course work alone.

II Decision to publish rests with author.
Published by the author or the Institute.

III No restrictions on Library access.
Not available for personal loan or inter-library loan.

IV Copyright is held by the author.
Author's permission is required for copying.
Photocopy or microform copy is made available
for purchase with the author's permission.
Not available for exchange.

V   Listed in the Library's catalogue.

VI -

006 QUEENSLAND INSTITUTE OF TECHNOLOGY

Chief Librarian
Library
GPO Box 2434, Brisbane, Queensland, 4001

I   Master's (8,7,8); Postgraduate diploma (15,14,26).
Most theses are deposited in the Library. Decision
rests with Academic Boards.

II Not published.

III Library access, personal loan and inter-library loan
are subject to conditions set by the author.

IV Copyright is held by the author.
Author's permission is required for copying.
Not available for exchange.

V   Listed in the Library's catalogue.

VI One copy of each Master's thesis is also deposited
with the National Library of Australia.

007 ROYAL MELBOURNE INSTITUTE OF TECHNOLOGY

Senior Librarian - Reader Services
Central Library
376-392 Swanston Street,
Melbourne, Victoria 3000

I   Master's (0,0,2).
Degrees were previously awarded by the Victoria
Institute of Colleges.
Has only been awarding its own higher degrees
since 1981. At April 1982, 88 students were
enrolled in Master's degrees by research.

II Not published.

III Library access is subject to conditions of
confidentiality.
Personal loan is not permitted.
Not available for inter-library loan.

IV Author's permission is required for copying.
Not available for purchase or exchange.

V   Listed in the Library's catalogue and in the *Union list of higher degree theses in Australian university libraries.*

VI Regulations on access and availability are incomplete except for those relating to confidentiality and may be modified at a future date.

008   SOUTH AUSTRALIAN INSTITUTE OF TECHNOLOGY

Chief Librarian
Central Library
PO Box 1, Ingle Farm South Australia 5098

I   Master's (3,6,9); Postgraduate diploma (8,10,0). Thesis is awarded 20% of total credit for Postgraduate diploma.
Two copies of Master's theses are requested, one each for deposit and loan.
Some are held in schools/departments only.

II -

III Legal opinion is being sought on Library consultation.
Available for personal loan. Microform would be made available for inter-library loan in Australia and abroad.

IV No special restrictions on copying.
Not available for exchange.

V   Listed in the Library's catalogue.
Some theses are indexed in *AESIS (Australian Earth Sciences Information System).*
Entered on the *Australian Bibliographic Network (ABN).*

VI -

009   SWINBURNE INSTITUTE OF TECHNOLOGY

Swinburne Librarian
Swinburne Library
PO Box 218, Hawthorn
Victoria 3122

I   Master's (theses in progress); Postgraduate diploma.
Master's degrees were previously awarded by the Victoria Institute of Colleges - to May 1981.
Postgraduate diplomas for deposit are selected by teaching departments.
Not all are presented.

II   Not published.

III No restrictions on Library access.
     Personal loan is not permitted.
     Photocopy is available for inter-library loan within
     Australia only.

IV   Copyright is held by the Institute.
     No restrictions on copying.
     Not available for purchase or exchange.

V   Listed in the Library's catalogue.

VI   -

010   TASMANIAN COLLEGE OF ADVANCED EDUCATION

Chief Librarian
Library
PO Box 1214, Launceston
Tasmania 7250

I   Master's (8,6,6); Postgraduate diploma (19,8,11).
     Master's thesis is awarded 15% of total course
     credit.
     Postgraduate thesis is awarded 20% of total course
     credit and no copies are deposited.

II   Not published.

III No restrictions on Library access.
     Available for personal loan.
     Photocopy is available for inter-library loan within
     Australia and abroad.

IV   Copyright is held by the author.
     No special restrictions on copying.
     Not available for purchase or exchange.

V   Listed in a special catalogue of theses.

VI   -

011   VICTORIAN COLLEGE OF PHARMACY LIMITED

Librarian
C.L. Butchers Memorial Library
381 Royal Parade
Melbourne, Victoria 3052

I   Doctoral (3,1,1,); Master's (6,7,6).
     Also offers Postgraduate diplomas by course work
     alone.

II   Theses are not published.

III No restrictions on library access.
     Available for personal loan and inter-library loan
     subject to the approval of the Head of School.

IV Copyright is held by the College.
Permission of the Head of School is required for copying.
Not available for purchase or exchange.

V Listed in the Library's catalogue and *Publications and communications of the Victorian College of Pharmacy Limited.*

VI -

012 WESTERN AUSTRALIAN INSTITUTE OF TECHNOLOGY

Circulation Librarian
T.L. Robertson Library
Kent Street, Bentley, Western Australia 6102

I Master's (7,23,24); Postgraduate diploma (32,51,60). (Approximate).
Percentage of credit for thesis varies for both courses.
One hardcopy and a microfiche copy of Master's theses are deposited. Deposit of Postgraduate diploma theses depends on the department.

II Not published.

III No restrictions on Library access.
Microfiche copy is available for personal loan and inter-library loan within Australia and abroad.

IV Copyright is held by the author.
Library has dispensation to make theses available for scholarly purposes and to provide copies.
Copying as prescribed by the Australian Copyright Act 1981. Copying of up to 100% is permitted for research.
Microfiche copy would be available for purchase and exchange. Catalogue cards would not be included.

V Listed in the Library's catalogue and its annual report.
Details are sent for inclusion in the *Union list of higher degree theses in Australian Libraries.*

VI Theses not held in the Library may be available from teaching departments. Enquire through the Library.

CANADA

013 **COLLÈGE DOMINICAIN DE PHILOSOPHIE ET DE THÉOLOGIE**

Dean's Office
Faculty of Theology
96 Empress Avenue, Ottawa, Ontario KIR 792

I   Doctoral (0,1,0); Master's (1,2,1); Postgraduate diploma (0,0,1).
All entail course work and thesis.
Deposited in the Dean's Office, not the Library.

II   Some authors have theses published by various publishing houses.

III   Consultation and loan only with the author's permission.

IV   Copyright is held by the author.
Author's permission is required for copying.
Not available for purchase or exchange.

V   Not listed in the Library's catalogue.
A list of theses is sent to the Public Archives.

VI   -

014 **COLLEGE OF EMMANUEL & ST. CHAD**

President
College of Emmanuel & St. Chad Library
1337 College Drive, Saskatoon,
Saskatchewan, S7N OW6

I   Master's (1,0,0)
Master's is by course work and thesis.

II   Not published.

III   No restrictions on Library access.
Not available for personal loan.
Photocopy is available for inter-library loan within Canada only.

IV   Copyright is held by the institution.
No special restrictions on copying.
Prepared to exchange theses with catalogue cards included.

V   Listed in the Library's catalogue.

VI   -

015 NOVA SCOTIA COLLEGE OF ART AND DESIGN

Librarian
Nova Scotia College of Art and Design Library
5163 Duke Street, Halifax,
Nova Scotia, B3J 3J6

I Master's (0,1,0; 3 in 1982)
   Thesis constitutes 27.3% of total course credit.
   2 copies are deposited.

II Published by the Art Education Department in
    photocopied format.

III No restrictions on Library access.
     Available for personal loan.
     Photocopy is available for inter-library loan within
     Canada and abroad.

IV No special restrictions on copying.
    Author can apply for copyright.
    Prepared to exchange theses with cataloguing
    information included.

V Listed in the Library's catalogue.

VI -

016 REGIS COLLEGE

Librarian
15 St. Mary Street
Toronto, Ontario, M44 2R5

I Doctoral; Master's; Postgraduate diploma.
   All are offered by course work and thesis.
   Doctoral and Master's theses are deposited.

II Not published.

III No restrictions on Library access.
     Available for personal loan and inter-library loan
     within Canada.

IV No special restrictions on copying.
    No available for purchase or exchange.

V Listed in the Library's catalogue.

VI -

017 ## SAINT PAUL UNIVERSITY

Executive Secretary
Research Centre
223 Main Street, Ottawa, Ontario K15 1C4

I   Doctoral (4,4,4); Master's (1,1,1).
Doctoral and Master's degrees are by course work
and thesis.
Also offers Master's by course work and seminar
paper.
2 copies are deposited.

II   Theses may be published by the author.

III   No restrictions on Library access.
Available for personal loan. A photocopy is
available on inter-library loan within Canada and
abroad.

IV   Copyright is held by the author.
No restrictions on copying.
Copies are not available for purchase.
Prepared to exchange theses, with catalogue cards
included.

V   Listed in the Library's catalogue and a special
catalogue of theses. Also listed in the national
bibliography - *Canadiana* and a national thesis
bibliography.

VI   Copies are deposited with the National Library.

CHILE

018 FACULTAD LATINOAMERICANA DE CIENCAS SOCIALES, PROGRAMA SANTIAGO

Director
Casilla 3213
Correo Central, Santiago

I   Master's (0,15,0).
Master's Degree programme ceased after 1983. An extraordinary Master's degree was held in 1978/80 in conjunction with CELADE (Latin American Centre for Demography).

II   Not published.

III   No restrictions on Library access.
Original is available for inter-library loan within Chile only.

IV   Copyright is held by the author and the institution. No restrictions on copying.

V   Listed in the Library's catalogue.

VI   -

DENMARK

Centralised Thesis Exchange

A centralised exchange service for theses operates from the:

I.D.E. : Danish Institute for International Exchange of Publications
Amaliegade 38
DK 1256, Copenhagen K, Denmark

019   DANMARKS LAERERHØJSKOLE (Royal Danish School of Educational Studies)

Librarian
Danmarks Laererhøjskoles Bibliotek
Emdrupvej 101, DK-2400, Copenhagen NV

I   Doctoral (2,1,2).
Also offers a Master's degree and Postgraduate diploma by course work alone.
3 copies are deposited.

II   Published by the institution and various Danish publishers.

III   No restrictions on Library access.
Original is available for personal loan and inter-library loan within Denmark and abroad.

IV   Copyright is held by the author.
General copyright restrictions apply.
Not available for purchase or exchange.

V   Listed in the Library's catalogue and the national bibliography. Abstracted in *Dissertation abstracts international, C.*

VI   -

020   HANDELSHØJSKOLEN I ÅRHUS (Arhus School of Business Administration, Economics and Modern Languages)

Library
Fuglesangsalle 4, DK 821U. Århus V

I   Doctoral (0,0,1); Master's (112,94,121);
Doctorate and Postgraduate diplomas are by thesis alone.
2 copies are deposited.

II   Published by various publishers.

III   No restriction on Library access.
Original is available for personal loan and inter-library loan within Denmark and abroad.

IV Copyright is held by the author.
Copyright law applies.
Prepared to exchange theses. Contact the I.D.E. :
Danish Institute for International Exchange of
Publications.

V Listed in the Library's catalogue and the national
bibliography - *Dansk bogfortegnelse.*

IV Copies of theses are exchanged with universities
and institutes of higher education.

021   HANDELSHØJSKOLEN I KØBENHAVN
(Copenhagen School of Economics and Business
Administration)

Handelshøjskolens Bibliotek
Julius Thomsens Plads 10, DK 1925,
Copenhagen V

I Doctoral (1,0,0); Licentiate (2,1,3); Master's
(114,133,160)
Doctoral degree is by thesis alone. Licentiate and
Masters are by course work and thesis.
Postgraduate diplomas by course work are also
offered.
5 copies of Doctoral theses and 1 of Licentiates are
deposited.

II Doctoral theses are usually published by
Erhversvsokonomisk Forlag S/I, an independent,
non-profit organisation.

III No restrictions on Library access.
Original is available for personal loan and inter-
library loan within Denmark and abroad.

IV Copyright is held by the author.
Author's permission is required for copying.
Copyright law applies.
Available for purchase and exchange :
contact the I.D.E. : Danish Institute for
International Exchange of Publications. Catalogue
cards would not be included.

V Listed in the Library's catalogue and the national
bibliography. Listed in *Handelshøjskolen i
København Beretnung 19xx /yy* (Annual report - in
Danish).

VI Copies of Doctoral theses are deposited in the
Royal Library and most university libraries.

022 **KØBENHAVNS TANDLAEGEHØJSHOLE** (Royal Dental College)

Royal Dental College Library
Vennelyst Boulevard, DK 8000. Århus C

I Doctoral (1,0,1); Master's (1,1,1).
Doctoral degree is by thesis alone.
Master's is by course work and thesis (50% credit for thesis).

II Published by the author.

III No restrictions on library access.
Original or photocopy is available for personal loan and inter-library loan within Denmark and abroad.

IV Copyright is held by the author.
No special restrictions on copying.
Not available for exchange.

V Listed in the Library's catalogue and the national bibliography.

VI Copies are deposited in the State and University Library, Århus.

FINLAND

023 **HELSINGIN KAUPPAKORKEAKOULU** (Helsinki School of Economics)

Head Librarian
Helsinki School of Economics Library
Runeberginkatu 22-24, SF-00100, Helsinki 10

I Doctoral (3,4,3); Master's (132,123,126); Licenciate (6,3,7).
Doctoral degree and Master's are by course work and thesis.
3 copies of a Doctoral thesis and 1 of a Master's are deposited.

II Published by the Helsinki School of Economics and Business Administration.
Few copies are published.

III No restrictions on Library access.
Master's theses are for Library reference only.
Only Doctoral and Licentiate theses are available for personal loan and inter-library loan within Finland and abroad.

IV Copyright is held by the author.
Copyright law applies.
Theses are available for purchase and exchange.
Catalogue cards would be included in exchanges.
Contact the centralised exchange service :
Tieteellisen Kirjallisuuden Vaihtokeskus.

V Listed in the Library's catalogue and a special catalogue of Master's theses.
Doctoral and Licentiate theses are listed in the national bibliography. From 1981 also listed in *Dissertation Abstracts International, C.*

VI Older Doctoral and Licentiate theses are not always available.

024 **KUOPION KORKEAKOULU** (Kuopio University)

Acquisitions Librarian
Kuopio University Library
POB 138, SP-70101, Kuopio 10

I Doctoral (8,5,16); Master's (25,29,44); Postgraduate diploma (2,9,3).
All are by course work and thesis. Doctoral thesis receives 75% of total credit, Masters, 15% and Postgraduate diploma 50%.
100 copies of a Doctoral thesis are deposited.

II Doctoral theses are published by the University.

III No restriction on library access if thesis is cited.
Available for personal loan.
Original is available for inter-library loan within
Finland and abroad.

IV Copyright is held by author.
Journals and the University hold copyright when
theses are published by them.
Available for purchase and exchange, not
including catalogue cards.

V Listed in the Library's catalogue, a special thesis
catalogue, the national bibliography and
Dissertation abstracts international, C.

VI Theses are exchanged with 50 Finnish and 20
foreign universities and institutions.

025   **VASAAN KORKEAKOULU** (University of Vaasa)

Interurban Loans Department
Vaasa University Library
Raastuvankatu 33, 65100 Vaasa 10

I Doctoral (0,0,1); Master's (13,26,49).
Doctorate is by thesis alone.
Master's is by course work and thesis (50% of total
credit).

II Published by the University in its series
Proceedings of research papers.

III No restrictions on library access.
Available for personal loan and inter-library loan
within Finland (original) and abroad (photocopy).

IV Copyright is held by the author.
No restrictions on copying.
Doctoral theses are available for purchase and
available for exchange if published in the series
Proceedings of research papers. Catalogue cards
would not be included.

V Listed in the Library's catalogue, the Finnish
national bibliography *Suomen Kirjallisuus* (doctoral
theses only) and *Scanp : Scandinavian periodicals
index in economics and business.*

VI Published Doctoral theses are sent to all Finnish
university libraries and some abroad.

FRANCE

026 CENTRE SÈVRES

Bibliothèque du Centre Sèvres
35 Rue de Sèvres, 75006, Paris

I   Doctoral; Master's (5,2,9)
    Offers Doctorate by thesis alone and by Master's
    thesis and course work.
    Offers Licentiate by course work alone.
    Theses are deposited in a special Library.

II Doctoral theses are occasionally published by the
    author.

III No restrictions on library access.
    Original is available for personal loan and inter-
    library loan within France and abroad.

IV No special restrictions on copying other than the
    cost.
    Not available for purchase.
    Prepared to offer theses for exchange.

V   Listed in a special catalogue of theses.

VI -

027 ÉCOLE CENTRALE DE LYON

Service 3e Cycle
Centre d'Information
BP 163 - 69131 Ecully Cedex

I   Doctoral; Diplôme d'études approfondies.

II -

III No restrictions on library access.
    Original is available for personal loan and inter-
    library loan within France and abroad.

IV No special restrictions on copying.
    Not available for purchase.

V   -

VI Theses are also deposited in the libraries of the
    University of Lyon I; University of St. Étienne;
    Institut National Polytechnique de Grenoble;
    CNRS (PASCAL database); NASA database;
    ESRIN database, Italy.

028 **INSTITUT INDUSTRIEL DU NORD**

Centre de Documentation "François Laurent"
BP 48 59651 Villeneuve d'Ascq Cedex

I   Doctoral (2,2,4).
   Degree is by thesis alone.
   A minimum of 2 copies are deposited.

II Published by the Institute.

III No restrictions on Library access.

IV Copyright is held by the author.

V   -

VI Theses are exchanged with French and foreign
   universities.

029 **INSTITUT SUPÉRIEUR DES MATÉRIAUX ET DE LA
CONSTRUCTION MÉCHANIQUE**

3 Rue Fernand Hainaut
93407 Saint - Ouen Cedex

I   Doctoral; Postgraduate diploma.

II -

III No restrictions on library access.
   Available for personal loan.
   Photocopy is available for inter-library loan within
   France and abroad.

IV No special restrictions on copying.
   Available for purchase and exchange. Contact the
   centralised exchange service CNRS : Centre
   National de la Recherche Scientifique.

V   Listed in the Library's catalogue and the THESA
   database.

VI One copy is deposited with the CNRS Central
   Library.

THE FEDERAL REPUBLIC OF GERMANY (BRD)

030 EBERHARD - KARLS UNIVERSITÄT TÜBINGEN

Dissertationen - und Tauschstelle der Universitätsbibliothek
74 Tübingen, Wilhelmstrasse 32

I Doctoral (506,547,433); Master's; both degrees are by thesis alone.
150 copies of a typed thesis are deposited or 30 copies of a published thesis.

II Published in printed or photocopied format by private publishers.

III No restrictions on library access.
Original is available for personal loan and inter-library loan within the Federal Republic and abroad.

IV Copyright is generally held by the author, except in cases of a publisher's contract.
No restriction on copying.
Microfilm copies of typed theses may be sold.
Available for exchange with catalogue cards included. In some cases free copies may be sent to non-exchange libraries.

V Published theses are listed in the Library's catalogue. All are listed in a special catalogue of theses.
Listed in *Dissertationenverzeichnis der Tübinger Doktorarbeiten* and *Deutsche Bibliographie, Reihe H.*

VI Ccpies are deposited with the DeutscheBibliothek Frankfurt.

031 HOCHSCHULE DER BUNDESWEHR, HAMBURG
(University of the Armed Forces)

Bibliothek der Hochschule der Bundeswehr
Holstenhofweg 85, D-2000 Hamburg 70

I Doctoral (4,11,23); Postgraduate diploma (252,371,434).

II Published by the author in printed format or microform.

III No restrictions on library access.
Original or photocopy is available for personal loan and inter-library loan within the Federal Republic and abroad.

IV Copyright is held by the author.
No restrictions on copying.
Not available for purchase.
Prepared to exchange theses. Catalogue cards would not be included.

V Listed in the Library's catalogue and the *Deutsche Bibliographie, Reihe H.* Also listed in *Deutsche Nationalbibliographie, Reihe C.*

VI Copies of Doctoral theses are deposited in most German university libraries.

032 HOCHSCHULE HILDESHEIM

Assistant Librarian
Hochschulbibliothek
Marienburger Platz 22, 3200 Hildesheim

I Doctoral (20,5,3)
Degree is by thesis alone.
150 copies are deposited.

II Published by private houses.

III No restrictions on library access.
Original is available for personal loan and inter-library loan within the Federal Republic and abroad.

IV Copyright is held by the institution.
No restriction on copying. 5-10 copies are made available as donations to institutions or individuals. Available for exchange with catalogue cards included.

V Listed in the Library's catalogue and the *Deutsche Bibliographie, Reihe H.* Also listed in *Zeitschrift für Pädagogik.*

VI Copies are sent to many German libraries, all European national libraries and the Library of Congress.

033 PÄDAGOGISCHE HOCHSCHULE FLENSBURG
(College of Education, Flensburg)

Präsident der Pädagogischen Hochschule Flensburg
Bibliothek
Murwiker Strasse 77, D2390 Flensburg

I Doctoral (1,0,0); Postgraduate diploma (7,2,3).
Both entail course work and thesis.
Doctoral theses 150 copies deposited.
Postgraduate diplomas - 2 copies deposited.

II Published by the author.

III No restrictions on library access.
Original is available for personal loan and inter-library loan within the Fedral Republic and abroad.

IV Copyright is held by the author.
No special restrictions on copying.
Not available for purchase.

Available for exchange with catalogue cards included.

V   Listed in the Library's catalogue, a special catalogue of theses and the *Deutsche Bibliographie, Reihe H.*

VI   Copies are also deposited in the Deutsche Bibliothek, Frankfurt; Deutsche Bucherei, Leipzig; Osterreichische Nationalbibliothek, Vienna; Schweizerische Landesbibliothek, Bern.

034   TECHNISCHE UNIVERSITÄT CLAUSTHAL

Universitätsbibliothek
Leibnizstrasse 2, D3392 Clausthal - Zellerfeld

I   Doctoral.
2 copies are deposited.

II   -

III   No restrictions on library access.
Available for personal loan.
Available on inter-library loan within the Federal Republic and abroad.

IV   Copyright is held by the author and the institution.
No special restrictions on copying.
Available for exchange.

V   Listed in the Library's catalogue and a special catalogue of theses.

VI   Abstracts are made available by the Deutsche Bibliothek.

035   THEOLOGISCHE FAKULTÄT TRIER

Bibliotheksdirektor
Bibliothek des Bischoflichen Priesterseminars Trier
Jesuitenstrasse 13, D5500 Trier

I   Doctoral; (3,2,3); Habilitation (1,0,0); Licentiate (2,0,0).
Doctoral and Licentiate degrees are by course work and thesis (60% credit for thesis).
2 copies are deposited.

II   Must be published by the author.

III   No restrictions on library access.
Original is available for personal loan and inter-library loan within the Federal Republic and abroad.

IV   Copyright is held by the author.
No special restrictions on copying.
Available for purchase.
Not available for exchange.

V   Listed in the Library's catalogue and a special
     catalogue of theses.
     Listed in *Archiv für Mittelrheinische
     Kirchengeschichte.*

VI   -

036   UNIVERSITÄT OLDENBURG

*Bibliotheks-und Informationssystem der Universität
Oldenburg
Uhlhornsweg, 2900 Oldenburg*

I   Doctoral (4,3,8).
     Degree is by thesis and oral examination.
     150 copies are deposited.

II   Most theses are unpublished except for a few
     published by small publishing houses.

III No restrictions on library access.
     Available for personal loan.
     Original is available for inter-library loan within the
     Federal Republic and abroad.

IV   Copyright is held by the author.
     No special restrictions on copying.
     Not available for purchase.
     Available for exchange with catalogue cards
     included.

V   Listed in the Library's catalogue and a special
     catalogue of theses.
     Listed in the *Deutsche Bibliographie. Reihe H.*

VI   -

INDIA

037 INDIAN INSTITUTE OF TECHNOLOGY, MADRAS

Librarian
Institute Library
Madras 600 036

I   Doctoral (55,52,78); Master's (43,44,40).
Both are by thesis alone.
Also offers Master's degrees by course work.

II Not published.

III No restrictions on library access.
Available for personal loan.
Photocopy is available for inter-library loan within
India and abroad.

IV Copyright is held by the institution.
No restrictions on copying.
Not available for purchase.
Contact the Librarian for information on
exchanges.

V   Listed in the Library's catalogue, a special
catalogue of theses, the national bibliography and
in the Institute's publication *Abstracts of Ph.D. theses.*

VI -

ISRAEL

038   WEIZMANN INSTITUTE OF SCIENCE

Acquisitions Librarian
Wix Library
P.O.B. 26, Rehevot 76 100

I   Doctoral (66,41,66); Master's (71,40,43).
Students are mainly evaluated on research work
but course work is required.

II   Not published.
Papers on research work may be published in
international journals.

III No restrictions on library access.
Available for personal loan.
Photocopy is available for inter-library loan within
Israel and abroad.

IV   Copyright is held by the author.
No special restrictions on copying.
Not available for purchase or exchange.

V   Listed in a special catalogue of theses.

VI   -

ITALY

039 PONTIFICIA UNIVERSITÀ SAN TOMMASO

University Library
Largo Angelicum 1,00184 Rome

I Doctoral (22,20,31).
50 copies are deposited.

II Published by the author.

III No restrictions on library access.
Not available for personal loan or inter-library loan.

IV Copyright is held by the author.
No special restrictions on copying.
Available for purchase.
Not available for exchange.

V Listed in the Library's catalogue.

VI Copies are deposited in some Rome libraries.

040 PONTIFICIUM INSTITUTUM BIBLICUM

Secretary - General
Secretariate of the Institute
Via della Pilotta 25 - 00187, Rome

I Doctoral (9,5,9).
Thesis is awarded 53% of total course credit.
Offers Licence by course work alone.

II Publication is arranged by the author.

III Prior to publication, library access is available with the author's permission.
Not available for personal loan or inter-library loan.

IV Copyright is held by the author.
Prior to publication, a photocopy can be supplied, with the author's permission.
Prepared to offer copies for exchange on a limited basis only.

V Published theses are listed in the Library's catalogue.
Listed in *Acta Pontificii Instituti Biblici, Elencus Bibliographicus Biblicus.*

VI 50 copies are distributed to affiliated universities.

041   **UNIVERSITÀ PONTIFICIA SALESIANA** (Salesian
Pontifical University)

Registrar
General Secretariat
p. Atenco Salesiano 1 - 00139, Rome

I   Doctoral (9,10,8); Master's (85,76,67);
Postgraduate diploma (5,10,21).
5 copies are deposited. 3 copies of Postgraduate
theses are deposited.

II   Published by the author.

III   Library access is available in a consulting room.
Not available for personal loan or inter-library loan.

IV   Copyright is held by the author.
No special restrictions on copying.
Available for exchange with catalogue cards
included.

V   Listed in the Library's catalogue and a special
catalogue of theses. Listed in the review
Salesianum.

VI   -

IVORY COAST

042   INSTITUT CATHOLIQUE DE L'AFRIQUE DE L'OUEST

Bibliothèque
08 BP22, Abidjan 08

I   Doctoral (no awards as yet); Licence (7,13,10).
5 copies of a Doctoral thesis will be deposited.

II   Not generally published.
Occasionally published in the review *Savanes et forêts*

III No restrictions on library access.
Available for personal loan.
Generally not available for inter-library loan.

IV   Copyright is held by the author.
No restrictions on copying.
Photocopy would be available for exchange.

V   Listed in the Library's catalogue.

VI   -

JAPAN

043   BAIKA JOSHI DAIGAKU (Baika Women's College)

Curator
Baika Women's College Library
2-19-5 Shukunosho, Ibaraki-shi, Osaka 567

I   Master's (8,6,6)
Thesis is required but no credit is given.
25 copies are deposited.

II   Not published.

III   No restrictions on library access.
Not available for personal loan or inter-library loan.

IV   Copyright is held by the institution.
Institution's permission is required for copying.
Not available for purchase or exchange.

V   Listed in a special catalogue of theses.

VI   -

044   OTARU SHOKA DAIGAKU (Otaru University of Commerce)

Reference Division
Otaru University of Commerce Library
3-5-21 Midori Otaru-Shi, 047 Hokkaido

I   Master's (3,0,1)

II   Not published.

III   No restrictions on library access.
Not available for personal loan.
Photocopy is available for inter-library loan within Japan and abroad.

IV   Copyright is held by the institution.
No special restrictions on copying.
Available for purchase.
Not available for exchange.

V   Listed in the Library's catalogue.

VI   -

045   **TOKYO SUISAN DAIGAKU** (Tokyo University of Fisheries)

Director of Library
Library
Konan 4-5-7, Minato-Ku, Tokyo 108

I   Master's (50,45,35).
Thesis is awarded 30% of total course credit.

II   Not published.

III   No restrictions on library access.
Not available for personal loan or inter-library loan.

IV   Copyright is held by the author.
Permission of Library Director is required for copying.
Not available for purchase or exchange.

V   Listed in a special catalogue of theses.

VI   -

KENYA

046 **INTERNATIONAL UNIVERSITY - AFRICA**

Library of the International University - Africa
PO Box 14634, Nairobi

I   Master's (13,22,15).
    2-3 copies are deposited.

II Not published.

III Library access is available to Postgraduate
    students and above.
    Not available for personal loan or inter-library loan.
    A photocopy will be supplied with the author's
    permission.

IV Copyright is held by the author.
    Author's permission is required for copying.
    Not available for exchange.

V   Listed in the Library's catalogue and a special
    catalogue of theses.

VI -

NETHERLANDS

047   INTERNATIONAAL INSTITUUT VOOR LUCHTKAARTERING EN AARDKUNDE (ITC) (International Institute for Aerial Survey and Earth Sciences)

Librarian
Library
PO Box 6, 7500 AA Enschede

I   Master's (12,22,29).
Degree is by course work and thesis.

II   Not published.

III   No restrictions on library access.
Not available for personal loan or inter-library loan.

IV   Copyright is held by the author.
Author's permission is required for copying.
Not available for purchase or exchange.

V   Listed in the Library's catalogue.

VI   -

048   KONINKLIJK INSTITUUT VOOR DE TROPEN (Royal Tropical Institute)

Central Library
Mauritskade 63, 1092 AD Amsterdam

I   Master's (0,18,0).
The International Course on Health Development is offered every even year.
The 3 best theses are chosen for deposit in the Library.
Thesis is awarded 25% of total credit.

II   Not published.

III   No restrictions on library access.
Original is available for personal loan and inter-library loan within the Netherlands and abroad.

IV   Copyright is held by the author.
No special restrictions on copying.
Not available for purchase or exchange.

V   Listed in the Library's catalogue.

VI   -

NORWAY

049   STICHTING INTERNATIONAAL INSTITUUT VOOR SOCIALE STUDIEN (Institute of Social Studies)

Librarian
Library
PO Box 90733, 2509LS The Hague

I   Doctoral (from 1983); Master's (49,47,44).
Master's thesis is awarded 40% of total course credit.
2 copies are deposited.
Also offers Postgraduate diplomas by course work.

III   No restrictions on library access.
Not available for personal loan or inter-library loan.

IV   Copyright is held by the Institute.
Copying is not permitted.
Not available for purchase or exchange.

V   Listed in the Library's catalogue.

VI   The above relates to Master's theses only.
Policies on Doctoral theses are to be decided.

050   ARKITEKTHØGSKOLEN I OSLO (Oslo School of Architecture)

Oslo School of Architecture Library
PO Box 6768, St. Olavs Plass, Oslo 1

I   Doctoral (None yet awarded).

II   Not to be published.

III   No restrictions on library access.
Will not be available for personal loan.
Original will be available for inter-library loan within Norway only.

IV   Copyright details have not yet been decided.
Will not be available for exchange.

V   Will be listed in the Library's catalogue and the national bibliography.

VI   -

051   NORGES HANDLESHØGSKOLE (Norwegian School of Economics and Business Administration)

Librarian
Norwegian School of Economics and Business
Administration Library
Helleveien 30, 5035 Bergen Sandviken

I   Doctoral (2,1,2); Master's (4,3,5);

Postgraduate diploma (138,160,135); Lisensiatgrad (1,0,1).
Master's thesis is optional.
2 copies of all theses are deposited.

II Seldom published.

III No restrictions on library access.
Original is available for personal loan and inter-library loan within Norway and abroad.

IV Copyright is held by the author.
Not available for purchase.
Doctoral theses are exchanged with many libraries and institutions. Catalogue cards are not included.

V Listed in the Library's catalogue and a special catalogue of theses. If published, they are included in the national bibliography.
Postgraduate diploma theses are listed in the bibliography *NHHB : NHH - Studentenes utredninger ved sivilokonomstudiets annen avdeling.*

VI -

052 NORGES IDRETTSCHØGSKOLE (Norwegian College of Physical Education and Sport)

Library
PB 40, Kringsja, Oslo 8

I Master's (20,9,3).
Thesis is awarded 50% of total course credit.
3-5 copies are deposited.

II Not published.

III No restrictions on library access.
Original is available for personal loan and inter-library loan within Norway and abroad.

IV Copyright is held by the author.
No special restrictions on copying.
Not available for purchase.
Limited exchanges offered, perhaps with catalogue cards.

V Listed in a special catalogue of theses and *Norwegian sports literature* (annual).

VI -

053 **NORGES VETERINAERHØGSKOLE** (Norwegian College of Veterinary Medicine)

Library
PO Box 8146 Dep, Oslo 1

I Doctoral (3,4,7); Dr. Scientiarum (8,9,11).
3 copies of Doctoral and 5 of Dr. Scientiarum theses are deposited.
Dr. Scientiarum is by thesis and course work.

II Published in printed format.

III No restrictions on library access.
Original is available for personal loan and inter-library loan within Norway and abroad.

IV Copyright is held by the author.
Copying is restricted to one copy.

V Listed in the Library's catalogue.
Doctoral theses are listed in the national bibliography.
Listed in *Dissertation abstracts international, C.*

VI Theses are also deposited at the Royal University Library, Oslo.

PERU

054 **ESCUELA DE ADMINISTRACIÓN DE NEGOCIOS PARA GRADUADOS** (Graduate School of Business Administration)

Jefe, Division de Documentación Información Y Proyectos Específicos
Centro de Documentación, A.P 1846, Lima 100

I Master's (16,19,18).
Master's is by course work and thesis which is compulsory.

II Not published.

III Library access only to staff and Master's graduates.
Available for personal loan.
Not available for inter-library loan.

IV Copyright is held by the author.
No special restrictions on copying.
Not available for purchase or exchange.

V Listed in a special catalogue of theses.

VI -

PHILIPPINES

055 LEYTE INSTITUTE OF TECHNOLOGY

Head, Library Services
Leyte Institute of Technology Library
Salazar Street, Tacloban City 7101

I   Master's (3,5,7).
    Degree is by course work and thesis.

II Not published.

III No restrictions on library access.
    Original is available for personal loan and inter-
    library loan within the Philippines.

IV Copyright is held by the Institute.
    No special restrictions on copying.
    Not available for purchase or exchange.

V   Listed in the Library's catalogue.
    Abstracts are published in the Institute's
    publication.
    Divine Word University lists the theses in a
    published thesis catalogue.

VI Copies are deposited in the National Library.

056 LUZON COLLEGES

Graduate School Library
Perez Blvd, Dagupan City

I   Master's (20,18,15).
    Degree is by course work and thesis.

II Not published.

III For library reference only.

IV Copyright is held by the author.
    Available for purchase.
    Available for exchange with catalogue cards
    included.

V   Listed in the Library's catalogue and a special
    catalogue of theses.

VI Copies are deposited with the Library of the
    Ministry of Education, Culture and Sports.
    The National Library provides a thesis exchange
    service.

057 PHILIPPINE UNION COLLEGE

Library Director
Leslie Hardinge Library
PO Box 1834, Manila

I Master's.
Degree is by course work and thesis.
1-2 copies are deposited.

II Not published.

III No restrictions on library access.
Not available for inter-library loan.

IV Copyright is held by the author.
Permission is required for copying.
Not available for exchange.

V Listed in the Library's catalogue, the national bibliography and the national theses bibliography.

VI Copies are deposited with the Library of the Ministry of Education Culture and Sport.

058 TECHNOLOGICAL UNIVERSITY OF THE PHILIPPINES

University Librarian
Graduate School Library
Ayala Blvd, Ermita, Manila 2801

I Doctoral (0,1,0); Master's (37,14,13).
Thesis is awarded 20% of Doctoral degree and 18.5% of Master's.
2 copies are deposited.
Offers Postgraduate diplomas by course work only.

II Published in the *Graduate School journal.*

III Library access is restricted.
Not available for personal loan or inter-library loan.

IV Copyright is held by the author and the institution.
No special restrictions on copying.
Not available for purchase or exchange.

V Listed in the Library's catalogue.

VI Copies are deposited with the Library of the Ministry of Education, Culture and Sports.

059   WEST VISAYAS STATE COLLEGE

Dean, Graduate School
West Visayas State College Library
La Paz, Iloilo City

I   Doctoral (no awards as yet); Master's (14,28,25).
     Thesis is awarded 16% of total credit for Doctoral
     degree and 14% of Master's.

II   Not published.

III No restrictions on library access.
     Available for library reference only.

IV   No restrictions on copying.
     A photocopy of the thesis would be provided if
     copying costs are paid by the requesting
     institution.
     Not available for exchange.

V   Listed in the Library's catalogue of theses and the
     national bibliography.
     Abstracted in the *Graduate School journal.*

VI   Copies are deposited with the Library of the
     Ministry of Education, Culture and Sports.

POLAND

060 **AKADEMIA ECONOMICZNA W. POZNANIU**
(Academy of Economics)

Director
Biblioteka Główna
ul. Marchlewskiego 146/150 Poznań

I   Doctoral (21,20,20); Postgraduate diploma
(227,107,189); Habilitation (3,3,10).

II Published by the Academy's publishing house.

III Access to Doctoral theses requires the consent of
the author or Vice-president for Scientific Affairs.
Not available for personal loan.

IV Copyright is held by the author.
Permission for copying is required from the author
or Vice-president for Scientific Affairs.
Not available for exchange.

V   Listed in a special catalogue of theses.
Listed in *Informator o zakonczonych pracach
naukowych.*

VI -

061 **AKADEMIA MEDYCZNA** (Medical Academy)

Biblioteka Główna
ul. SW. Anny 3, 31-008 Krakow

I   Doctoral (68,45,34).
1-2 theses are presented annually by candidates.

II Not published.

III No restrictions on library access.
Not available for personal loan.
Original is available for inter-library loan within
Poland only.

IV Copyright is held by the author and the Academy.
Not available for purchase or exchange.

V   Listed in the Library's catalogue, a special
catalogue of theses and in *Wykaz zakonczonych
prac naukowych, Warsąw.*

VI Copies are automatically deposited with CINTE
(Centrum Informacji Nawkowej, Technicznej i
Ekonomicznej), Warsaw and the Central Medical
Library.

062   **AKADEMIA MEDYCZNA** (Medical Academy)

Director
Biblioteka Główna
Muszynskiego 2, 90-151 Łódź

I   Doctoral (43,35,53); Habilitation (7,13,14).
Both are by course work and thesis.

II Not published.

III For library reference only.
Original is avilable for inter-library loan within Poland and abroad.

IV Copyright is held by the author.
No copying is permitted.
Not available for purchase or exchange.

V Listed in the Library's catalogue and a special catalogue of theses.
Doctoral theses are listed in *Biuletyn Głównej Biblioteki Lekarskiej.*
Habilitation theses abstracted in specialist journals.

VI Copies are automatically deposited with the Główna Biblioteka Lekarska, Warsaw.

063   **AKADEMIA MEDYCZNA** (Medical Academy)

Chief of the Department of Medical Information
Main Library
ul. Łakowa 1. Poznań

I   Doctoral (77,64,51); Habilitation (12,6,4)
Both degrees are by thesis alone.

II Published by the Academy in *Poznańskie roczniki medyczne.*

III No restrictions on library access.
Not available for personal loan.
Original is available for inter-library loan within Poland only.

IV Copyright is held by the author.
No copying is permitted.
Not available for purchase or exchange.

V Listed in a special catalogue of theses and *Katalog rozpraw doktorskich habilitacyjnych.*

VI Deposited in the Central Medical Library Warsaw.

064 AKADEMIA ROLNICZO-TECHNICZNA W OLSZTYNIE (Academy of Agricultural Technology)

Librarian
Biblioteka Główna
10-957 Olsztyn-Kortowo

I   Doctoral (76,79,55).
Offers Postgraduate diplomas by course work alone.

II Not published.

III No restrictions on library access.
Not available for personal loan.
Original is available for inter-library loan within Poland and abroad.

IV Copyright is held by the author.
No special restrictions on copying.
Not available for purchase or exchange.

V   Listed in a special catalogue of theses.
Listed in *Informator o zakończonych pracach naukowych.*

VI -

065 AKADEMIA ROLNICZA WE WROCLAAWIU (Academy of Agriculture)

Director
Main Library
50-375 Wroclaw, ul C. Norwida 25

I   Doctoral (52,45,39).
Also offers Postgraduate diplomas by course work alone.

II Published by the Academy and publishing houses.

III Author's permission is required for library access.
Original and photocopy are available for inter-library loan within Poland and abroad.

IV Copyright is held by the author.
Author's permission is required for copying.

V   Listed in a special catalogue of theses.
Published theses are listed in *Informator o Zakończonych pracach naukowych.*

VI -

066 AKADEMIA TECHNICZNO-ROLNICZA (Academy of Agriculture and Technology)

Biblioteka Główna Akademeii
Techniczno-Rolniczej im J.J. Sniadeckich
u1. prof. Sylwestra Kaliskiego nr.7,
85-763 Bydgoszcz

I   Doctoral (9,10,16).
    Degree is by thesis alone.
    No automatic deposit.

II Published by the Academy.

III No restrictions on library access.
    Not available for personal loan.
    Original is available for inter-library loan within
    Poland only.

IV Copyright is held by the Academy.
    Copying is restricted.
    Not available for purchase.
    Available for exchange.

V   Listed in a special catalogue of theses.

VI -

067 **AKADEMIA WYCHOWANIA FIZYCZNEGO WE
WROCLAWIU** (Academy of Physical Education in
Wroclaw)

Director
Biblioteka Główna
u1. Banacha 11, 51-617 Wroclaw

I   Doctoral (7,4,5).
    Degree is by thesis alone.

II Published in the Academy's *Rozprawy Naukowe.*

III No restrictions on library access.
    Original is available for personal loan and inter-
    library loan within Poland and abroad.

IV Copyright is held by the author.
    Not available for purchase or exchange.

V   Listed in a special catalogue of theses.
    Also listed in a publication of the Centre of
    Scientific, Technical and Economical Information
    (CINTE) and a bibliography of the Academy of
    Physical Education, Cracow.

VI -

068 **POLITECHNIKA SWIETOKRZYSKA** (Technical
University of the Holy Cross)

Librarian
Biblioteka Główna
A1. Tysiaclecia PP7. 25-314. Kielce

I   Doctoral (5,3,5);
    Degree is by course work and thesis.
    Theses are held in individual school archives and
    are accessible on request through the Library.

II   Not published.

III Available for library reference only.
     Available for inter-library loan within Poland and
     abroad for use within the library only.

IV   Copyright is held by the author.
     No special restrictions on copying.
     Not available for purchase or exchange.

V   Listed in a special catalogue of theses and the
     thesis bibliography *Informator o zakończonych
     pracach naukowych.*

VI   -

**069   SLASKA AKADEMIA MEDYCZNA IM L.
WARYNSKIEGO** (L. Warynski Silesian Medical
Academy)

*Biblioteka Główna
ul. Poniatowskiego 15, 40-492 Katowice*

I   Doctoral (50,67,51); Postgraduate diploma (3,8,5).
     2 copies are deposited.

II   Published by the National Institution of Medical
     Editions (Parstwowy Zaktad Wydawnictw
     Lekarskich).

III No restrictions on library access.
     Not available for personal loan.
     Photocopy is available for inter-library loan within
     Poland and abroad, with the author's consent.

IV   Copyright is held by the author.
     No special restrictions on copying.
     Not available for purchase or exchange.

V   Listed in the Library's catalogue and a special
     catalogue of theses. Listed in *Katalog rozpraw
     doktorskich i habilitacyjnych* and *Informator o
     zakończonych pracach naukowych*

VI   Copies are deposited in Glowna Biblioteka
     Lekarska, Warsaw. Contact: CINTE 00-950 Warsaw
     for thesis exchange service.

070   WYŻSZA SZKOŁA PEDAGOGICZNA (Graduate
College of Education)

*Biblioteka Główna-Oddzial Informacji Naukowej
Biblioteka Główna Wyzszej Szkoly Pedagogicznej W Opolu
45-052 Opole, ul. Oleska 48*

I   Doctoral (20,17,9); Postgraduate diploma
     (1063,990,973)
     Postgraduate diploma is by thesis alone.

II   Published by the College and other publishers.

III No restrictions on library access.
Original is available for personal loan and inter-library loan within Poland and abroad. Photocopy may also be supplied.

IV Copyright is held by the author and the College.
No restrictions on copying.
Not available for purchase or exchange.

V Listed in the Library's catalogue and a special catalogue of theses.
Listed in *Katalog rozpraw doktorskich, informator o zakończonych pracach naukowo - Badawczych.*

VI -

071 WYŻSZA SZKOŁA PEDAGOGICZNA IM EDUKACJI NARODOWEJ (Graduate College of Education in Honour of the National Commission for Education)
Head, Research Information Unit
Central Library of the Higher Pedagogical School
u1. Podchorazych 2, 30 - 084 Kraków

I Doctoral (30,49,37); Habilitation (5,6,1).
Copies of Habilitation theses are not deposited but purchased where a need is seen.

II Published by the College's publishing house or other Polish publishers.

III Permission for library access is required from the author or the professor conferring the degree.
Not available for personal loan.
Original is available for inter-library loan within Poland and abroad (the latter with the permission of the author or professor).

IV Copyright is held by the author and professor conferring the degree whose permission must be obtained for copying.
Not available for purchase.
Habilitation theses would be available for exchange. For a list contact Wydawnictwo Naukowe WSP, u1. Karmelicka 41, Kraków.

V Listed in the Library's catalogue and the national bibliography. Listed in the *Annotated catalogue of Doctoral dissertations. 1946-1973. Cracow, 1975.*

VI -

SOUTH AFRICA

072   CAPE TECHNIKON

Librarian
John Garlick Library
PO Box 652, Cape Town 8000

I   Doctoral (5 expected in 1985); Master's (50 in
1982).
2 copies are deposited. Master's degree is offered
by thesis alone, thesis and course work and course
work alone.

II   -

III No restrictions on library access.
Not available for personal loan.
Original is available for inter-library loan within
South Africa, a photocopy for loan abroad.

IV   No special restrictions on copying.
Not available for exchange.

V   Listed in the Library's catalogue.

VI   Copies are deposited with the libraries of the
Council for Scientific and Industrial Research, the
Human Sciences Research Council and the
Department of National Education.

073   PORT ELIZABETH TECHNIKON

The Librarian
Sanlam Library
Private Bag X6011, Port Elizabeth 6001

I   National Higher Diploma, National Diploma in
Technology, National Laureatus in Technology.
No thesis for these courses have yet been
presented.
2 copies of the National Diploma in Technology
thesis would be deposited.

II   Author would be free to have the thesis published.

III Access would only be restricted when the author
requires confidentiality.
Will be available for personal loan.
A photocopy will be available for inter-library loan
within South Africa and abroad.

IV   Copyright will be held by the Technikon.
Normal copyright law applies.
A photocopy of the thesis will be provided at cost.
Prepared to offer theses for exchange at cost.
Catalogue cards would be included.

V Listed in the Library's catalogue.

VI Copies are deposited with the libraries of the Council for Scientific and Industrial Research, the Human Sciences Research Council and the Department of National Education.

074 PRETORIA TECHNIKON

Head, Library
Pretoria Technikon Library
420 Church Street East
Pretoria 0002

I National Diploma in Technology (15,36,18); Laureatus.
2 copies are deposited.

II Not published.

III No restrictions on library access.
Original is available for personal loan and inter-library loan within South Africa and abroad.

IV Copyright is held by the author.
No special restrictions on copying.
Not available for purchase.
Available for exchange - without catalogue cards.

V Listed in the Library's catalogue.

VI Theses are deposited with the Department of National Education, the Human Sciences Research Council and the Council for Scientific and Industrial Research.

075 WITWATERSRAND TECHNIKON

Senior Librarian
Technikon Witwatersrand Library
Po Box 3293, Johannesburg 2000

I National Higher Diploma; National Diploma in Technology.
2 copies would be deposited.

II -

III Restrictions on library access would depend on the nature of the research.

IV Not decided but the Technikon will probably hold copyright.
Copying of parts may be allowed.
Would be prepared to exchange theses.

V Will be listed in the Library's catalogue and the *Bulletin of the Human Sciences Research Council.*

VI -

SPAIN

076 FACULTAD DE TEOLOGIA

Sr. Bibliotecario
Biblioteca, Martinez del Campo 10, Burgos

I   Doctoral (1 in 1982); Master's (3,4,2).
Doctoral degree is by thesis alone.
Master's thesis receives 70% of total course credit.

II   Published by the author.

III   Access to Doctoral theses requires author's
permission. Not available for personal loan or
inter-library loan.

IV   Copyright is held by the author.
Author's permission is required for copying.
A photocopy could be supplied with the author's
permission.
Not available for exchange.

V   Listed in the Library's catalogue.
Listed in *Memoria del Curso.*

VI   -

077 FACULTAD DE TEOLOGIA DE GRANADA

Sr. Bibliotecario
Biblioteca Facultad Teologia
Apartado 2002, Granada

I   Doctoral (1,1,0); Master's (3,4,5).
Both degrees are by course work and thesis.
Library deposit of Master's thesis depends on their
value.

II   Published by Biblioteca Teologica Granadina.

III   No restrictions on library access.
Not available for personal loan or inter-library loan.

IV   Copyright is held by the institution.
No special restrictions on copying.
Available for purchase if in the Library collection.
Photocopy is also available.
Not available for exchange.

V   Listed in a special catalogue of theses and the
Faculty's own publication.

VI   Theses are exchanged with state universities.

**078 FACULTAD DE TEOLOGIA DEL NORTE DE ESPAÑA
SEDE DE VITORIA**

Bibliotecario Jefe
Biblioteca del Seminario Diocesano de Vitoria
Apartado 86, Vitoria

I   Doctoral (0,0,1); Master's (0,3,0).
Thesis is awarded 50% of total credit for both
degrees.

II Doctoral theses are published by the author or the
institution.

III No restrictions on library access.
Not available for personal loan or inter-library loan.

IV Copyright is held by the author.
No special restrictions on copying.
Not available for exchange.

V   Listed in the Library's catalogue.

VI Copies are deposited in the Library of the Facultad
de Teologia del Norte de Espana, Sede de Burgos.

SWITZERLAND

Centralised Thesis Exchange

A centralised exchange service for theses operates from the:

Schweizerische Dissertationszentrale
Jupiterstrasse 15
CH 3000. Bern 15. Switzerland

079 ÉCOLE POLYTECHNIQUE FÉDÉRALE DE LAUSANNE (Swiss Federal Institute of Technology of Lausanne)

Secrétaire Général Bibliothèque Centrale
CH 1015. Lausanne

I   Doctoral (29,38,33); Diplom
    'Travaux de diplom' are not deposited.
    2 copies of doctoral theses are deposited.

II Some are published in printed or microfiche
    format. Authors often use the Presses
    Polytechniques Romandes as publishers.

III No restrictions on library access.
    Available for personal loan and inter-library loan
    within Switzerland and abroad (most often in
    microfiche format).

IV Copyright is held by the author.
    Subject to copyright restrictions.
    One copy per reader.
    Longer theses are available for purchase.
    Microfilm copies of others will be donated.
    Prepared to offer theses on exchange, without
    catalogue cards.

V   Listed in the Library's catalogue, a special
    catalogue of theses, the national bibliography and
    the *Jahrverzeichnis der Schweizerischen
    Hochschulschriften/Catalogue des écrits
    academiques suisses.*

VI -

080 THEOLOGISCHE FAKULTÄT LUZERN

Fakultätsversammlung
Zentralbibliothek
Sempacherstrasse 10, CH 6003 Luzern

I   Doctoral (2,4,3); State Diploma (24,20,17);
    Habilitation.
    40 copies of Doctoral theses are deposited.

II Doctoral theses are published in printed or microfiche format.

III No restrictions on library access.
    Photocopy is available for personal loan and inter-library loan within Switzerland and abroad.

IV Copyright is held by the institution.
    Copying is not permitted.
    Available for purchase and exchange.

V   Listed in the Library's catalogue and the national bibliography.

VI Theses are deposited in Swiss university libraries.

UNITED KINGDOM OF GREAT BRITAIN AND NORTHERN IRELAND

General Information

Degrees undertaken by British polytechnics are awarded by the Council for National Academic Awards (CNAA). From 1980, the CNAA has forwarded theses of successful Master's and Doctoral candidates to the British Library Lending Division for microfilming.

The theses are listed in the BLLD's - *British reports, translations and theses.*

081   BRIGHTON POLYTECHNIC

Head of Learning Resources
Department of Learning Resources
Moulsecoomb, Brighton BN2 4GJ, England

I   Doctoral.
Degree is by thesis alone.

II   Not published.

III   No restrictions on library access.
Not available for personal loan.
Photocopy and microform are available for inter-library loan within the U.K. and abroad.

IV   Copyright is held by the author.
No special restrictions on copying.
Not available for purchase or exchange.

V   Listed in the Library's catalogue.
Listed in Aslib - *Index to theses ...* and BLLD - *British reports, translations and theses.*

VI   -

082   CAMBORNE SCHOOL OF MINES

Librarian
Library
Trevenson, Pool, Redruth
Cornwall TR15 3SE England

I   Doctoral (1,1,2); Master's (2,1,7); Postgraduate diploma (2,1,0).
Thesis is awarded 33% of Master's degree and 75% of Postgraduate diploma.

II   Not published.

III   Occasional 2 year restrictions on theses which include confidential company information.
Not available for personal loan.

Original is available for inter-library loan within the U.K. only.

IV Copyright is held by the author.
Author's permission is required for copying.
Not available for purchase or exchange.

V Listed in the Library's catalogue.

VI Theses are deposited with the British Library Lending Division and listed in its publications.

083 CITY OF LONDON POLYTECHNIC

Library and Learning Resources Service
Calcutta House. Old Castle Street
London. E1 7NT. England

I Doctoral (1,9,14); Master's (49,60,76); Postgraduate diploma

II Not published.

III Access may be restricted if confidentiality has been registered with the CNAA.
Not available for personal loan or inter-library loan.
Available through the British Library Lending Division.

IV Copyright is held by the Council for National Academic Awards (CNAA) whose permission is required for copying.
Not available for purchase or exchange.

V Listed in the Library's catalogue.
Listed in Aslib - *Index to theses.*

VI Copies are deposited with the British Library Lending Division.

084 COLEG LLYFRGELLWR CYMRU (College of Librarianship, Wales)

Librarian
Library
Llanbadarn Fawr, Aberystwyth, Dyfed SY23 3AS, Wales

I Master's (2,5,5)
Degree is by thesis alone and by course work and thesis.

II Not published.

III No restrictions on library access.
Original is available for inter-library loan within the U.K. only.

IV Copyright is held by the author.
Author's permission is required for copying.
Available for purchase.
Not available for exchange.

V   Listed in the Library's catalogue and a special
catalogue of theses.
Listed in the Library Association's publications
CABLIS and *RADIALS bulletin.*

VI Copies are deposited with the Library of the
University College of Wales and the National
Library of Wales.

085   HATFIELD POLYTECHNIC

Head of Reader Services
Library
College Lane, Hatfield, Hertfordshire, England

I   Doctoral (2,8,7); Master's (2,7,6).
Doctoral degree is by thesis alone.
Master's is by course work and thesis.

II Published in printed format.

III Theses sponsored by external organisations may
require a 'confidential' cover.
Available for personal loan.
Original (rarely) or microform copy is available for
inter-library loan within the U.K. and abroad.

IV Copyright is held by the author and the institution.
Copyright Act and / or confidentiality restrictions
apply to copying.
Possibly prepared to exchange theses.

V   Listed in a special catalogue of theses.
Listed in Aslib - *Index to theses ...* and BLLD - *British*
reports, translations and theses.

VI Abstracts are sent to the British Library Lending
Division.

086   KINGSTON POLYTECHNIC

Chief Librarian
Learning Resources : Library
Penrhyn Road, Kingston upon Thames, Surrey, KT1 2EE
England

I   Doctoral; Master's.
Both degrees are by thesis alone.
Not all theses are deposited.
Also offers Master's and Postgraduate diplomas by
course work alone.

II May be published subsequently by commercial
publishers.

III Available for library reference only.
Not available for personal loan.
Available for inter-library loan within the U.K. only.

IV   Copyright is held by the author.
Author's permission is required for copying.
Not available for purchase or exchange.

V   Listed in Aslib - *Index to theses ...*

VI -

087   LEEDS POLYTECHNIC

Librarian
Polytechnic Library
Calverley Street, Leeds, LS1 3HE, England

I   Doctoral (0,1,1); Master's (2,0,1).
Both are by thesis alone.
Automatic deposit of theses since 1981.

II   Not published.

III   No restrictions on library access.
Original is available for inter-library loan within the
U.K. only.

IV   Copyright holder has not yet been determined.
Copyright 'fair dealing' restrictions apply.
Not available for purchase or exchange.

V   Listed in the Library's catalogue.

VI -

088   LIVERPOOL POLYTECHNIC

Librarian in Charge, Inter-Library Loans Unit
Library
Byrom Street, Liverpool L3 3AF, England

I   Doctoral (16,19,14); Master's (17,7,4).

II   Not published.

III   Available for library reference only. Theses are
held in the site library for the department in which
the work was undertaken.
Not available for personal loan.
Original is available for inter-library loan within the
U.K. and abroad.

IV   Copyright is held by the author.
Author's permission is required for copying.
Copies may be sold with the author's permission.
Not available for exchange.

V   Listed in the Library's catalogue.
Listed in Aslib - *Index to theses ...* and BLLD - *British
reports, translations and theses.*

VI   British Library Lending Division has received
copies of theses since 1981.

089 LONDON BIBLE COLLEGE

Librarian
Library
Green Lane. Northwood. Middlesex HA6 2UW. England

I Doctoral; Master's (1,1,0).
   Both degrees are by thesis alone.
   Master's is also awarded by course work and
   thesis (25% of total credit).

II Not published.

III No restrictions on library access.
    Not available for personal loan or inter-library loan.
    Available through the British Library Lending
    Division.

IV Copyright is held by the author.
   No special restrictions on copying.
   Not available for purchase or exchange.

V Listed in BLLD - *British reports, translations and
   theses.*

VI Microfilm copies of Doctoral theses are deposited
   with the British Library Lending Division.

090 LUTON COLLEGE OF HIGHER EDUCATION

Librarian
College Library
Park Square, Luton, Bedfordshire, England

I Doctoral (2,2,2); Master's (2,2,2).
   Both degrees are by thesis alone.

II Not published.

III Available for library reference only.
    Not available for personal loan.
    Original is available for inter-library loan within the
    U.K. only. Also available from the British Library
    Lending Division.

IV Copyright is held by the author.
   Author's permission is required for copying.
   Not available for exchange.

V Listed in the Library's catalogue and the Aslib -
   Index to theses ...

VI Copies are sent to the British Library Lending
   Division.

091   MIDDLESEX POLYTECHNIC

Head of Library Services
Central Library
Bounds Green Road, London N11 2NQ, England

I   Doctoral (approx. 5,5,5); Master's (approx.
50,50,50); Postgraduate diploma (approx.
50,50,50).
All are by thesis alone.
Postgraduate diploma theses are not deposited.
Master's also by course work and thesis (approx.
33.3%).

II   Not published.

III   For library reference only. Theses are located in
the appropriate site library.
Not available for personal loan or inter-library loan.

IV   For Doctoral and Master's theses, copyright is held
by the author.
Normal copyright restrictions apply and
reasonable requests are considered.
Not available for exchange.

V   Listed in the Library's catalogue and the Aslib -
Index to theses ...

VI   -

092   OXFORD POLYTECHNIC

Librarian
Oxford Polytechnic Library
Headington, Oxford OX3 OBP, England

I   Doctoral (1,1,1); Master's (39,36,23).
Only town planning theses are deposited in the
Library.

II   Not published.

III   Theses are kept on closed access for library
reference only
Not available for personal loan.
Original or microform copy is available for inter-
library loan within the U.K. and abroad.

IV   Copyright is held by the author.
Librarian's permission is required for copying.
Not available for purchase or exchange.

V   Listed in Aslib - *Index to theses ...*
Town planning theses are listed in Greater London
Council - *Urban abstracts.*

VI   -

093 PAISLEY COLLEGE OF TECHNOLOGY

Librarian
Library
High Street, Paisley PA1 2BE, Scotland

I   Doctoral (4,4,6); Master's (0,3,2).
Both degrees are by thesis alone.

II   Not published.

III   Copyright declaration signature is required for consultation.
Not available for personal loan.
Available for inter-library loan within the U.K. and abroad.

IV   Copyright is held by the Council for National Academic Awards (CNAA).
Author's permission is required for copying.
Microform copy is available for purchase.
Not available for exchange.

V   Listed in the Library's catalogue.
Listed in *Dissertation abstracts international* and BLLD - *British reports, translations and theses.*

VI   Copies are sent to the British Library Lending Division.

094 PLYMOUTH POLYTECHNIC

Deputy Librarian
Library
Drake Circus, Plymouth PL4 8AA, England

I   Doctoral (9,10,6); Master's (15,11,3).
Doctoral degree is by thesis alone.
Master's is awarded by thesis and course work plus thesis (credited 40%).

II   -

III   Available for library reference only.
Not available for personal loan.
Photocopy or microfilm available for inter-library loan within the U.K. and abroad.

IV   Copyright is held by the author.
Reader must sign a copying declaration.
Not available for purchase or exchange.

V   Listed in the Library's catalogue and a special catalogue of theses.
Listed in Aslib - *Index to theses ...*
Doctoral theses are listed in BLLD - *British reports translations and theses.*

VI   -

095 THE POLYTECHNIC

Inter-Loans Assistant
Main Library. Queensgate Campus
Queensgate. Huddersfield, HD1 3DH. England

I   Doctoral (3,4,9); Master's (8,7,13).
Postgraduate diploma (1 in 1979).
Postgraduae diploma theses are not deposited.

II Not published.

III For library reference only.
Not available for personal loan.
Original is available for inter-library loan within the
U.K. and abroad.

IV Copyright is held by the author and the institution
whose permission is required for limited copying.
Available for purchase.
Not available for exchange.

V   Listed in the Library's catalogue and a special
catalogue of theses.
Listed in Aslib - *Index to theses ...*

VI -

096 POLYTECHNIC OF THE SOUTH BANK

Inter-library Loans Librarian
Library
Borough Road, London SE1 0AA, England

I   Doctoral (2,6,1); Master's (4,8,10); Postgraduate
diploma.
Master's and Postgraduate diploma are by course
work and thesis.

II Not published.

III No restrictions on library access.
Not available for personal loan.
Original is available for inter-library loan within the
U.K. and abroad.

IV Copyright is held by the author.
Author's permission is required for copying.
Not available for exchange.

V   Listed in the Library's catalogue and Aslib - *Index
to theses ...*

VI −

097 SHEFFIELD CITY POLYTECHNIC

Reader Services Librarian
Main Library
Pond Street, Sheffield, S1 1WB, England

I Doctoral; Master's.
Doctoral and Master's are by thesis alone. Master's and Postgraduate diplomas also by course work and thesis.

II Not published.

III For library reference only.
Not available for personal loan.
Original is available for inter-library loan within the U.K. and abroad (will consider individual cases).

IV Copyright is held by the author.
Not available for purchase or exchange.

V Listed in the Library's catalogue and a special catalogue of theses.
Doctoral theses are listed in Aslib - *Index to theses ...*

VI Doctoral theses are deposited with the British Library Lending Division.

098 THAMES POLYTECHNIC

Reader Services Librarian
Main Library
Wellington Street, London SW18 6PF, England

I Doctoral (7,9,8); Master's (49,38,41); Postgraduate diploma (14,32,16).
Postgraduate diplomas are not deposited.

II Not published.

III No restrictions on library access.
Not available for personal loan.
Original is available for inter-library loan within the U.K. and abroad.

IV Copyright is held by the author.
Brief extracts only may be copied for purposes of scholarship.
Not available for purchase or exchange.

V Listed in the Library's catalogue.

VI Copies are deposited with the British Library Lending Division.

099   ULSTER POLYTECHNIC

Librarian
Main Library
Shore Road, Newtownabbey, Co. Antrim BT37 0QB
Northern Ireland

I   Doctoral (1,4,4); Master's (1,3,3).
    Doctoral thesis is 25% of total course credit. Offers
    Postgraduate diploma by course work only.

II Not published.

III No restrictions unless 'confidential' - access may
    be restricted for 5 years.
    Available for personal loan.
    Original is available for inter-library loan within
    Northern Ireland.

IV Copyright is held by the author.
    Author's permission is required for copying.
    Not available for exchange.

V   Theses are listed in a special catalogue.
    Doctoral theses are listed in *Dissertation abstracts*
    international, C.

VI -

UNITED STATES

100 ADAMS STATE COLLEGE

Director
Adams State College Library
Alamosa, Colorado, 81102

I   Master's (116,112,114).
Most Master's are by course work alone.
A few require theses - approximately 13% of credit.
2 copies are deposited.

II   Not published.

III   No restrictions on library access.
Available for personal loan.
Original is available for inter-library loan within the
U.S.A. and abroad.

IV   Copyright is held by the author.
No special restrictions on copying.
Not available for purchase or exchange.

V   Listed in the Library's catalogue.

VI   -

101 ALBANY MEDICAL COLLEGE

Head. Technical Services
Schaffer Library of Health Sciences
47 New Scotland Avenue. Albany. New York 12208

I   Doctoral (7,7,6); Master's (0,3,4).
Both are by course work and thesis.

II   Published by University Microfilms.

III   Theses are held in a closed access area.
Not available for personal loan or inter-library loan.

IV   Copyright is held by the author of he/she chooses.
No special restrictions on copying.
Not available for purchase except through
University Microfilms.
Not available for exchange.

V   Listed in the Library's catalogue and *Dissertation
abstracts international.*

VI   -

102 AMERICAN CONSERVATORY OF MUSIC

Head Librarian
Hattstaedt Library
116 Michigan Avenue. Chicago. Illinois 60603

I   Doctoral (0,1,2).
Degree is by course work and thesis.

Offers Master's by course work alone.
Copies of Doctoral theses have been deposited
since 1980 only.

II Published in printed and microform format by
University Microfilms.

III No restrictions on library access.
Not available for personal loan or inter-library loan.

IV Copyright is held by the author.
No special restrictions on copying.
Available for purchase from University Microfilms.
Not available for exchange.

V   Listed in the Library's catalogue and recently in
Dissertation abstracts international.

VI -

103 AMERICAN GRADUATE SCHOOL OF INTERNATIONAL MANAGEMENT

Librarian
Barton Kyle Memorial Library
Thunderbird Campus, Glendale, Arizona 85306

I   Master's.
Degree is awarded by course work and thesis
(optional).

II Not published.

III No restrictions on library access.
Available for inter-library loan within the U.S.A.
only.

IV Copyright is held by the institution.
Not available for exchange.

V   Listed in the Library's catalogue.

VI -

104 ART CENTER COLLEGE OF DESIGN

James Lamont Fogg Memorial Library
1700 Lida Street, Pasadena, California 91103

I   Master's (1,2,2).
Degree is by course work and thesis.

II Not published.

III No restrictions on library access.
Available for personal loan.
Photocopy is available for inter-library loan within
the U.S.A. and abroad.

IV   Copyright is held by the institution.
No special restrictions on copying.
Available for purchase and exchange with
catalogue cards included.

V   Listed in the Library's catalogue and a special
catalogue of theses.

VI   -

105   AUGUSTANA COLLEGE

Inter-library Loans
Archives
Sioux Falls, South Dakota 57197

I   Master's (less than 20 in each year).
Theses are only deposited on the basis of a
departmental decision.

II   Not published.

III   For use within the Library only.
Photocopy is available for inter-library loan within
the U.S.A.

IV   Copyright is held by the institution.
Copright law restrictions apply.
Photocopy is available for purchase.
Not available for exchange.

V   Listed in the Library's catalogue.

VI   Some theses will be entered on the OCLC - Ohio
College Library Center data base.

106   BALTIMORE HEBREW COLLEGE

Director of the Library
Joseph Meyerhoff Library
5800 Park Heights Avenue, Baltimore
Maryland 21215

I   Doctoral; Master's (14,10,16).
Thesis is awarded 35% of total course credit for
Doctorate and 20% for Master's.

II   Not published.

III   No restrictions on library access.
Not available for personal loan or inter-library loan.

IV   Copyright is held by the author and the institution.
Copyright law applies.
Not available for purchase.

V   Listed in the Library's catalogue.

VI   -

70

107 BETHANY NAZARENE COLLEGE

Inter-Library Loans
R.T. Williams Learning Resources Center
4115 N.College, Bethany, Oklahoma 7300

I   Master's.
Thesis is optional and awarded 10% of credit.
Also deposited in the Dean's office.

II Not published.

III No restrictions on library access.
Not available for personal loan except when a
duplicate is available for loan from Dean's office.
Original is available for inter-library loan to special
seminary facilities.

IV Copyright is held by the author.
Not available for purchase or exchange.

V   Listed int he Library's catalogue and a special
catalogue of thesis.

VI Retrospective cataloguing is being carried out and
theses are being entered in the OCLC : Ohio
College Library Center data base.

108 BOSTON CONSERVATORY

Head Librarian
Albert Alphin Music Library
8 The Fenway, Boston
Massachusetts 02215

I   Master's (4,4,3).
2 copies are deposited.

II Photocopied and bound locally.

III Available for library reference only by
appointment.
Not available for personal loan or inter-library loan
except by special permission of the author and / or
Head Librarian.

IV Copyright is held by the author.
No copying of entire thesis or of a complete
chapter or section.
Not available for purchase or exchange.

V   Listed in the Library's catalogue.

VI Use of compositions for performance only by
arrangement with candidate composer.

109 BROOKLYN COLLEGE

Special Collections
Brooklyn College Library
Bedford Avenue and Avenue H, Brooklyn
New York 11210

I   Master's (61,47,67).

II Publishing may be arranged by the author.

III Restrictions on library access may be imposed by
    the author or the department.
    Not available for personal loan.
    Photocopy or duplicate is available for inter-library
    loan within the U.S.A. and abroad.

IV Copyright is held by the author.
    Photocopying restrictions may be imposed by the
    author. Credit must be given to author when using
    material.
    Available for purchase if not restricted.
    Not available for exchange.

V   Not currently listed in the Library's catalogue.
    (Were listed 1932-1973). An in-house author and
    departmental listing is maintained.
    Listed in *Master's theses in the pu·e and applied
    sciences accepted by colleges and universities of the
    United States and Canada.* edited by Wade H.
    Shafer.

VI -

110 BRYN MAWR COLLEGE

Head, Public Services
Canaday Library
Bryn Mawr, Pennsylvania 19406

I   Doctoral (38,46,43); Master's (126,123,131).
    Library acquires Master's theses in Science and
    Social Work only.

II Most are published by University Microfilms and
    some in journals.

III If not published, permission for access is required
    from the author or author's agent.
    Microform is available for personal loan.
    Available for inter-library loan within the U.S.A.
    and abroad.

IV Copyright is held by the author.
    Not available for purchase or exchange.

V   Listed in the Library's catalogue and by author in a
    special catalogue of theses.
    Abstracted in *Dissertation abstracts international.*

VI -

111   CALIFORNIA STATE COLLEGE, BAKERSFIELD

Reference Librarian
Library
9001 Stockdale Highway, Bakersfield
California 93309

I   Master's (25,20,35).
Degree is by course work and thesis or course
work alone.
2 copies are deposited.

II   Not published.

III   No restrictions on library access.
Available for personal loan.
Original is available for inter-library loan within the
U.S.A. and abroad.

IV   Copyright is held by the author.
Not available for purchase or exchange.

V   Listed in the Library's catalogue and a special
catalogue of theses.

VI   -

112   CALIFORNIA STATE COLLEGE, STANISLAUS

Head of Public Services
Library
801 W.Monte Vista Avenue
Turlock, California 95380

I   Master's (34 in 1980/81).
2 copies are deposited.

II   Published by University Microfilms.

III   No restrictions on library access.
Available for personal loan.
Original is available for inter-library loan within the
U.S.A. and abroad.

IV   Copyright is held by the author.
Not available for exchange.

V   Listed in the Library's catalogue and a special
catalogue of theses.
Some are abstracted in University Microfilms
Masters abstracts : catalog of selected masters theses
on microfilm.
Also listed in *Master's theses in education* and
Masters theses in the social sciences.

VI   -

113 CALVARY BIBLE COLLEGE

Head Librarian
Kroeker Library
Kansas City, Missouri 64147

I   Master's.
Thesis is 6% of total course credit.
2 copies are deposited.

II   Not published.

III   No restrictions on library access.
Available for personal loan.
Original or microform is available for inter-library loan within the U.S.A. and abroad.

IV   Copyright is held by the institution.
Copying restrictions decided on case-by-case basis.
Microform would be available for purchase.
Not available for exchange.

V   Listed in the Library's catalogue and a special catalogue of theses.

VI   -

114 CLARION STATE COLLEGE

Interlibrary Loan Office
Carlson Library
Clarion, 16214, Pennsylvania

I   Master's (9,5,5).
Theses are optional in 3 Master's programmes and worth 10% - 20% of total credit.
2 copies are deposited.

II   Not published.

III   Available for personal loan.
Original is available for inter-library loan within the U.S.A. and abroad.

IV   Not available for purchase or exchange.

V   Listed in the Library's catalogue.
Entered in the OCLC : Ohio College Library Center data base.

VI   –

115 CLEVELAND INSTITUTE OF MUSIC

Director of the Library
Library
11021 East Boulevard, Cleveland, Ohio 44106

I   Doctoral (3,1,1,); Master's (6,3,2).
'Documents' are awarded between 8% and 21% of total course credit.

II Not published.

III Available for library use only.
Not available for inter-library loan.

IV No legal copyright.
Limited photocopying is permitted.
Not available for purchase or exchange.

V Listed in the Library's catalogue.

VI -

116 COLGATE ROCHESTER DIVINITY SCHOOL

Circulation Co-ordinator
Ambrose Swasey Library
1100 S. Goodman Street, Rochester
New York 14620

I Doctoral (18,9,6); Master's (2,0,0).
Thesis is awarded 26% of credit for Doctorate and
15% for Masters. Also offers M.Divinity by course
work.
2 copies of Doctoral theses are deposited.

II Some theses are published.

III Available for library consultation only.
If a second copy is deposited, personal loan and
inter-library loan within the U.S.A. are available.

IV Copyright is held by the author.
Author's permission is required for copying.
Not available for purchase or exchange.

V Listed in the Library's catalogue and reported to
the Library of Congress for inclusion in the
National Union Catalogue.

VI -

117 COLLEGE OF NOTRE DAME

Notre Dame Library
1500 Ralston Avenue, Belmont, California 94002

I Master's (12,16,14); Montessori Diploma (20,25,10).
Thesis is 20% of total credit.
No automatic deposit. Some theses only are
acquired as gifts.

II Not published.

III No restrictions on library access.
Not available for personal loan.
Original is available for inter-library loan within the
U.S.A. only.

IV Copyright is held by the author.
No special restrictions on copying.
Not available for exchange.

V Listed in the Library's catalogue.

VI -

118 COLUMBIA THEOLOGICAL SEMINARY

Reader Services Librarian
John Bolow Campbell Library
701 Columbia Drive, Decatur, Georgia 30031

I Doctoral (11,17,16); Master's (1,3,1).
2 copies are deposited.

II Not published.

III No restrictions on library access.
Original is available for personal loan and inter-library loan.

IV Copyright is held by the institution.
Author's permission is required for copying.
Not available for purchase or exchange.

V Listed in the Library's catalogue and a special catalogue of theses.

VI -

119 CONCORDIA TEACHERS COLLEGE

Director of Library Services
Link Library
800 N. Columbia. Seward. Nebraska 68434

I Master's (0,1,0).
Thesis is optional.

II Author may publish.

III No restrictions on library access.
Available for personal loan. Photocopy is available for inter-library loan within the U.S.A. and abroad.

IV Copyright is held by the author if he so chooses.
No restrictions on copying unless author retains copyright.
Photocopy would be made available if copying and shipping costs were paid.
Not available for exchange.

V Listed in the Library's catalogue.

VI -

120 CONCORDIA THEOLOGICAL SEMINARY

Library
6600 N. Clinton Street
Fort Wayne, Indiana

I   Master's (125,130,138).
2 copies are deposited.
Also offers Master's by course work alone.

II   Not published.

III   No restrictions on library access.
Available for personal loan and inter-library loan
within the U.S.A. and abroad.

IV   Copyright is held by the author.
No special restrictions on copying.
Available for purchase and exchange, including
catalogue cards.

V   Listed in the Library's catalogue and a special
catalogue of theses.

VI   -

121 CONNECTICUT COLLEGE

Reference Librarian
Library
New London, Connecticut 06320

I   Master's (27,33,27)

II   Not published.

III   No restrictions on library access.
Not available for personal loan.
Photocopy is available for inter-library loan within
the U.S.A. and abroad.

IV   Copyright is held by the author.
Not available for purchase or exchange.

V   Listed in the Library's catalogue.

VI   -

**122 COOPER UNION FOR THE ADVANCEMENT OF
SCIENCE AND ART**

Assistant Librarian
Cooper Union Library
41 Cooper Square, New York 10003

I   Master's (2,1,10).

II   Not published.

III   No restrictions on library access.
Not available for personal loan or inter-library loan.

IV No special restrictions on copying.
Not available for purchase or exchange. Available
through University Microfilms.

V Listed in a special catalogue of these and
Dissertation abstracts international.

VI -

123 COPPIN STATE COLLEGE

Reference Librarian
Parlett Longworth Moore Library
2500 West North Avenue, Baltimore
Maryland 21216

I Master's (111,75,36).

II Not published.

III No restrictions on library access.
Not available for personal loan or inter-library loan.

IV Copyright is held by the author.
No special restrictions on copying.
Not available for purchase.
Available through University Microfilms.

V Listed in the Library's catalogue.

VI -

124 DALLAS THEOLOGICAL SEMINARY

Director
Mosher Library
3909 Swiss Avenue, Dallas, Texas 75204

I Doctoral (10,8,9); Master's (195,214,243).
2 copies are deposited. Doctoral thesis is required
but not assessed. Master's thesis is awarded 33.3%
of total hours.

II Published by commercial publishers.

III No restrictions on library access.
Original or microform copy is available for
personal loan and inter-library loan within the
U.S.A. and abroad.

IV Copyright is held by the author.
Copying is to be carried out by the Library.
Available for purchase and exchange.

V Listed in the Library's catalogue and a special
catalogue of theses.
Listed in *Dissertation abstracts international.*

VI -

125 EASTERN OREGON STATE COLLEGE

Director of Libraries
Walter M. Pierce Library
LaGrande, Oregon 97850

I Master's (1 in 1979).
Most Master's have been awarded for a field study project and report. Master's by course work and thesis is also available.

II Not published.

III No restrictions on library access.
Not available for personal loan.
Photocopy is available for inter-library loan within the U.S.A. and abroad.

IV Copyright is held by the institution.
No special restrictions on copying.
Available for exchange with catalogue cards included.

V Listed in the Library's catalogue.

VI Original theses are held in a restricted collection and photocopies are produced at cost for circulation.

126 EMERSON COLLEGE

Periodicals Assistant
Library
100 Beacon Street, Boston
Massachusetts 021116

I Master's (27 in 1982, 29 in 1983).
2 copies usually deposited.

II May be published by authors.

III No restrictions on library access.
If a second copy exists, this is available for circulation and inter-library loan. Single copies may be consulted in the Library reference room.

IV Copyright is held by the author.
No special restrictions on copying.
Not available for purchase or exchange.

V Listed in the Library's catalogue.

VI -

127 FITCHBURG STATE COLLEGE

Assistant Reference Librarian
Fitchburg, Massachusetts 01420

I Master's.
No automatic deposit. Library Director has the
responsibility of procuring copies.

II Not published.

III No restrictions on library access.
Not available for personal loan or inter-library loan.

IV Copyright is held by the author.
Author's permission is required for copying.
Not available for exchange.

V Listed in the Library's catalogue and a special
catalogue of theses.

VI -

128 FRANCIS MARION COLLEGE

Interlibrary Loan Librarian
James A. Rogers Library
Florence, South Carolina 29501

I Master's (0,1,4).
Thesis is awarded 10% of total course credit.
Also offers Master's by course work alone.
2 copies are deposited.

II Not published.

III No restrictions on library access.
Original is available for personal loan and inter-
library loan within the U.S.A. and abroad.

IV Copyright is held by the author.
No special restrictions on copying.
Not available for purchase or exchange.

V Listed in the Library's catalogue.

VI -

129 FULLER THEOLOGICAL SEMINARY

Interlibrary Loan Librarian
McAlister Library
135 North Oakland Avenue
Pasadena, California 91101

I Doctoral (33 in 1982); Master's (11 in 1982);
Postgraduate diploma (65 in 1982).
2 copies are deposited.

II Published by University Microfilms from 1981.

III No restrictions on library access.
Available for personal loan to library card holders only.
Original is available for inter-library loan within the U.S.A. if not available through University Microfilms.

IV Copyright is held by the author.
Many are not copyright. The library neither grants nor denies permission to copy uncopyrighted theses.
Not available for exchange. Consult University Microfilms for purchase of post-1981 theses and McAlister Library for copies of others.

V Listed in the Library's catalogue and *Dissertation abstracts international.*

VI -

130 GANNON UNIVERSITY

Director
Nash Library
619 Sassafras Street, Erie, Pennsylvania 16541

I Master's (6,10,5).

II Not published.

III No restrictions on library access.
Available for personal loan.
Photocopy is available for inter-library loan in the U.S.A. and abroad.

IV Copyright is held by the institution.
No special restrictions on copying.
Not available for purchase.
Available for exchange, including catalogue listing cards.

V Listed in the Library's catalogue.

VI Theses are required in Engineering only.
Other courses require a research essay.

131 GEORGE WILLIAMS COLLEGE

Library
555, 31st Street, Downers Grove
Illinois 60515

I Master's (60,30,34).
Also offers Master's by course work alone.
2 copies are deposited.

II Not published.

III No restrictions on library access.
Available for personal loan.
Original is available for inter-library loan within the
U.S.A. and abroad.

IV Copyright is held by the author.
Not available for purchase.
Available for exchange without catalogue cards.

V Listed in the Library's catalogue and a special
catalogue of theses.
Listed in *Completed research in health, physical
education, recreation and dance* (Annual) and
*Bibliography of theses and dissertations in recreation
and parks* by Betty Vander Smissen, Pennsylvania
State University, 1970 and 1979 editions.

VI -

132 GEORGIA SOUTHERN COLLEGE

Director of Libraries
Library
Landrum Box 8073. Statesboro
Georgia 30460

I Master's (5,12,7).
Thesis is awarded 20% of total credit.
2 copies are deposited.
Also offers Master's by course work.

II Not published.

III No restrictions on library access.
Available for personal loan.
Photocopy is available for inter-library loan within
the U.S.A. and abroad.

IV Copyright is held by the author.
No special restrictions on copying.
Not available for exchange.

V Listed in the Library's catalogue and a special
catalogue of theses.

VI -

133 GOLDEN GATE BAPTIST THEOLOGICAL SEMINARY

Readers Services Librarian
Golden Gate Seminary Library
Strawberry Point. Mill Valley
California 94941

I Doctoral (4,5,8); Masters (0,1,3).
Thesis is awarded 12.5% of total credit for
Doctorate and 1/12 of credit for Master's.

Also offers Master's by course work.
2 copies are deposited.

II Not published.

III No restrictions on library access.
Available for personal loan.
Photocopy is available for inter-library loan within
the U.S.A. and abroad.

IV Prior permission is required for copying.
Not available for purchase or exchange.

V Listed in the Library's catalogue and a special
catalogue of theses.
Listed in *Dissertation abstracts international.*

IV Copyright is held by the author.

134   GRADUATE THEOLOGICAL UNION

Director
Library
2400 Ridge Road,
Berkeley, California 94709

I Doctoral (24,12,16); Master's 21,15,24);
Postgraduate diploma.

II Published in microform by University Microfilms.

III No restrictions on library access.
In some cases available for personal loan and
inter-library loan within the U.S.A. and abroad.

IV Copyright is held by the author.
No special restrictions on copying.
Not available for purchase or exchange.

V Listed in the Library's catalogue.

VI -

135   GRAND VALLEY STATE COLLEGES

Director
Zumberge Library
Allendale, Michigan 49401

I Master's.
Degree is offered by thesis alone, thesis and
course work and course work alone.

II Published by University Microfilms.

III No restrictions on library access.
Available for personal loan.
Photocopy is available for inter-library loan within
the U.S.A.

IV Copyright is held by the author.
Not available for purchase or exchange.

V   Listed in the Library's catalogue.
Listed in University Microfilms - *Master's abstracts.*

VI -

136   HERBERT H. LEHMAN COLLEGE

Chief, Reference Division,
Library
Bedford Park, Boulevard West
Bronx, New York 10468

I   Master's (60,65,95).
Degree is by course work and thesis.
2 copies are deposited.

II Not published.

III For library reference only.
Not available for personal loan or inter-library loan.

IV Copyright is held by the author.
Copying is not permitted.
Not available for purchase or exchange.

V   Listed in a special catalogue of theses.

VI -

137   HOLLINS COLLEGE

Librarian
Fishburn Library
Virginia 24020

I   Master's (28,26,33).
Thesis is awarded 20% of total course credit.

II Not published.

III No restrictions on library access.
Not available for personal loan.
Photocopy is available for inter-library loan within
the U.S.A. and abroad.

IV Copyright is held by the author.
Author's permission is required for copying.
Not available for purchase or exchange.

V   Listed in the Library's catalogue.

VI -

138   ILLINOIS COLLEGE OF OPTOMETRY

Librarian
Carl F. Shepard Memorial Library
3241 Michigan Avenue. Chicago. Illinois 60616

I   Doctoral (71,74,65).
Thesis is awarded 2% of total course credit.

II Published in various professional journals.

III No restrictions on library access.
Available for personal loan.
Original is available for inter-library loan within the
U.S.A. and abroad.

VI If published, publisher holds copyright. Otherwise,
usually not copyright.
Occasionally, restrictions on copying are
requested by the author.
Not available for purchase or exchange.

V Listed in the Library's catalogue.
List is sent annually to the American Optometric
Association and others on request.

VI -

139 INSTITUTE OF PAPER CHEMISTRY

Circulation Co-ordinator
Library
PO Box 1039, Appleton, Wisconsin 54912

I Doctoral (12,9,6); Master's (22,28,29).
Thesis is awarded 90% of total credit for Doctorate
and 20% for Master's.
2 copies are deposited.

II Doctoral theses are published internally and by
University Microfilms.

III Master's theses are for library reference only with
some exceptions considered.
Available for personal loan and inter-library loan
within the U.S.A. and abroad.

IV Copyright is held by the institution.
Available for purchase and exchange with
catalogue cards included. Also available through
University Microfilms.

V Listed in the Library's catalogue.
Listed in the *Abstract bulletin of the Institute of Paper
Chemistry.*

VI -

140 JACKSON STATE UNIVERSITY

Henry T. Sampson Library
1325 John R. Lynch Street
Jackson, Mississippi 39217

I Doctoral (4 in 198(2); Master's (49,52,56).
Thesis is awarded 20% of total credit for Doctorate
and 10% for Master's. Also offers Specialist in
Education degree for which a project is worth 10%
(33,22,19). Thesis is optional in some programmes.

II -

III No restrictions on library access.
Not available for personal loan.
Photocopy is available for inter-library loan within
the U.S.A. only.

IV Theses are not to be copied.
Not available for purchase or exchange.

V Listed in a special catalogue of theses.
Master's theses are listed in the *Negro educational review.*

VI -

141 JOHN JAY COLLEGE OF CRIMINAL JUSTICE

Library
445 West 59th Street, New York 10019

I Doctoral (new programme); Master's.
No credit for Doctoral thesis; Master's thesis is
awarded 16.6% of total course credit.

II Not published.

III No restrictions on library access.
Not available for personal loan.
Photocopy is available for inter-library loan.

IV Copyright is held by the author.
General copyright restrictions apply.
Not available for exchange.
Doctoral theses are available through University
Microfilms.

V Listed in the Library's catalogue and a special
catalogue of theses.

VI -

142 JOHN MARSHALL LAW SCHOOL

Director of Library Services
Library
315 S. Plymouth Crescent
Chicago, Illinois 60604

I Master's (4,6,8).
Thesis is awarded 12.5% of total course credit.
2 copies are deposited.

II Not published.

III Not available for personal loan or inter-library loan.

IV Copying is restricted.

V Not listed in the Library's catalogue or a special
catalogue of theses.

VI -

143 KEENE STATE COLLEGE

Reference Librarian
Mason Library
229 Main Street, Keene, New Hampshire 0343l

I Master's (4,4,5).
Majority of students elect to do the Master's by course work.

II Not published.

III No restrictions on library access.
Original is available for inter-library loan within the U.S.A. and a photocopy for loan abroad.

IV Copyright is held by the author.
No special restrictions on copying.
Not available for exchange.

V Listed in the Library's catalogue.
Incorporated in the OCLC : Ohio College Library Center data base.

VI -

144 KUTZTOWN UNIVERSITY OF THE PENNSYLVANIA SYSTEM OF HIGHER EDUCATION

Library Director
Rohrbach Library
Kutztown, Pennsylvania 19530

I Master's (6,8,13).
Thesis is optional in most Master's programmes and is awarded 20% of total credit when elected.
2 copies are deposited.

II Not published.

III No restrictions on library access.
Available for personal loan.
Original is available for inter-library loan within the U.S.A. and abroad.

IV Copyright is held by the author.
No special restrictions on copying.
Not available for purchase or exchange.

V Listed in the Library's catalogue and the OCLC : Ohio College Library Center data base.

VI -

145 LUTHERAN THEOLOGICAL SEMINARY AT PHILADELPHIA

Director
Krauth Memorial Library
7301 Germantown Avenue
Philadelphia. Pennsylvania 19119

I Doctoral (6,2,3); Master's (3,4,2).
Thesis is awarded 33% of total credit for Doctorate and 25% of credit for Master's. Also offers Master's by course work.

II May be published by the denominational press (Fortress) or serial publishers.

III For library reference only unless the author or heir has given permission for personal loan.
Photocopy or microform copy will be made available for inter-library loan with the author's permission.

IV Copyright is held by the author.
Author's permission is required for copying.
Duplicate copy will be made available for purchase with the author's permission.
Not available for exchange.

V Listed in the Library's catalogue.
Where appropriate is listed in the Lutheran Historical Conference bibliography.
D.Min. theses are indexed by the American Theological Library Association Religious Index Office.

VI -

146 MANCHESTER COLLEGE

Funderburg Library
North Manchester. Indiana 46962

I Master's (5,6,9).
Thesis is awarded 9% of total course credit.

II Not published.

III Not available for personal loan or inter-library loan.

IV Copyright is held by the author.
Author's permission or department head's permission is required for copying.
Not available for purchase or exchange.

V Listed in a special catalogue of theses.

VI -

147   MANHATTAN COLLEGE

Interlibrary Loan Librarian
Cardinal Hayes Library
Bronx. New York 10471

I   Master's (15,4,18).
Thesis is awarded 10% of total credit.
2 copies are deposited.

II   Not published.

III No restrictions on library access.
Original or photocopy is available for inter-library
loan within the U.S.A. and abroad.

IV   Not available for purchase or exchange.

V   Listed in the library's catalogue.

VI   -

148   MEDICAL COLLEGE OF GEORGIA

Librarian for Special Collections
Library
Laney Walker Boulevarde
Augusta. Georgia 30912

I   Doctoral (4,12,5); Master's (7,20,25).
2 copies are deposited.
Also offers Master's and Doctoral degrees by
course work alone.

II   Some theses have been deposited with University
Microfilms.

III Second copy is available for personal loan and
inter-library loan.

IV   Copyright is held by the author.
Extensive copying beyond 'fair use' requires the
author's permission.
Copies deposited with University Microfilms may
be purchased through them.
Not available for exchange.

V   Listed in the Library's catalogue and a Special
Collections shelf list.
Deposited theses are listed in *Dissertation abstracts*
international.

VI   -

149   MEDICAL COLLEGE OF WISCONSIN

Interlibrary Loan Librarian
Todd Wehr Library
8701 Watertown Plank Road
Box 26509, Milwaukee, Wisconsin 53226

I   Doctoral (4,12,10); Master's (2,7,15).
2 copies are usually deposited.

II   Not published.

III   No restrictions on library access.
If two copies are deposited, personal loan and inter-library loan within the U.S.A. and abroad would be available.

IV   Theses are not copyrighted.
No special restrictions on copying.
Not available for purchase or exchange.

V   Listed in the Library's catalogue.
Author may submit thesis for listing in *Dissertation abstracts international.*

VI   -

150   MEHARRY MEDICAL COLLEGE

Stanley L. Kresge Learning Resource Center
1005 18th Avenue North
Nashville, Tennessee 37208

I   Doctoral (4,2,2); Master's (0,0,1).
Thesis is awarded 40% of total course credit.

II   May be published in microform.

III   Available for library reference only.
Not available for personal loan or inter-library loan.

IV   Copyright is held by the author.
Entire theses may not be copied.
Not available for purchase or exchange.

V   Listed in the Library's catalogue and in *Dissertation abstracts international.*

VI   -

151   MILLS COLLEGE

User Services Librarian
Mills College Library
Oakland, California 94613

I   Master's (9,16,13).
Degree is offered by course work and thesis and Course work alone.
2 copies are deposited.

II   Not published.

III   Some theses are held in a locked area and must be
      requested.
      Available for personal loan.
      Original or microform is available for inter-library
      loan within the U.S.A. only.

IV   Copyright is held by the author.
      No special restrictions on copying.
      Not available for purchase or exchange.

V   Listed in the Library's catalogue.

VI   -

152   MILWAUKEE SCHOOL OF ENGINEERING

Associate Librarian
Walter Schroeder Library
500 East Kilborne Street, Milwaukee, Wisconsin 53201

I   Master's (17,8,11).
      Degree is by course work and thesis.
      Some theses are deposited according to the
      decision of the department's chairman.

II   Not published.

III Available for library use under direct supervision
      only.
      Available only to the School's students, Faculty
      and Alumni upon personal request.
      Not available for personal loan or inter-library loan.

IV   Copyright is held by the author.
      Photocopying is restricted.

V   Listed in a special catalogue of theses.

VI   -

153   MISSISSIPPI COLLEGE

Mississippi College Library
Box 127, Clinton, Mississippi 39056

I   Master's (10,13,11).
      Degree is by course work and thesis.
      2 copies are deposited.

II   Not published.

III Available for personal loan.
      Duplicate is available for inter-library loan within
      the U.S.A. and abroad.

IV   Copyright is held by the author.
      No special restrictions on copying.
      Not available for purchase or exchange.

V   Listed in the Library's catalogue.

VI   -

154 MONTANA COLLEGE OF MINERAL SCIENCE AND TECHNOLOGY

Reference Librarian
Library
Butte, Montana 59701

I Master's (10,8,15).
Degree is by course work and thesis.
2 copies are deposited.

II Publishing is arranged by the author.

III No restrictions on library access.
Available for personal loan when a second copy exists.
Original or photoocpy is available for inter-library loan within the U.S.A. and abroad.

IV Copyright holder varies.
No copying restrictions for research or scholarly purposes.*
Theses are exchanged on a voluntary basis with other state universities.

V Listed in the Library's catalogue and a special catalogue of theses.
Some are listed in *Bibliography and index of geology.*

VI -

155 MOUNT SAINT MARY'S COLLEGE

Library Director
Charles Willard Coe Memorial Library
12 001 Chalow Road
Los Angeles. California 90277

I Master's (6,11,4).
Thesis is awarded 10% of total course credit.

II Not published.

III No restrictions on library access.
Original is available for personal loan and inter-library loan within the U.S.A. and abroad.

IV Copyright is held by the author.
Several theses have copying restrictions requested.
Not available for exchange.

V Listed in the Library's catalogue.

VI -

156 NAZARENE THEOLOGICAL SEMINARY

William Broadhurst Library
1700 East Meyer Boulevard
Kansas City, Missouri 64131

I   Doctoral; Master's.
Thesis is awarded 20% of total credit for a
Doctorate. Only one Master's programme requires
a thesis (credit is approximately 5%).
2 copies are deposited.

II   Not published.

III   No restrictions on library access.
Available for personal loan.
Photocopy is available for inter-library loan within
the U.S.A. and abroad.

IV   Copyright is held by the author.
No special restrictions on copying.
Not available for purchase or exchange.

V   Listed in the Library's catalogue.
Listed in the OCLC : Ohio College Library Center
data base.
Listed in University Microfilms *American doctoral*
dissertations.

VI   -

157 NEW YORK INSTITUTE OF TECHNOLOGY

Reference Librarian
Schure Hall Library
Old Westbury, New York 11568

I   Master's (40,34,52).
Thesis is awarded 20% of total course credit when
this option is offered.
1 or 2 copies are deposited.

II   Not published.

III   No restrictions on library access.
Not available for personal loan.
Original or photocopy is available for inter-library
loan within the U.S.A. and abroad.

IV   Copyright is held by the author.
Limited copying with prior approval of the author.
Not available for purchase or exchange.

V   Listed in the Library's catalogue and a special
catalogue of theses.

VI   -

158 NORFOLK STATE UNIVERSITY

Reference Librarian
Lyman Beecher Brooks Library
2401 Corprew Avenue, Norfolk, Virginia 23504

I   Master's (13,9,13).
    Degree is by course work and thesis. Thesis is
    mandatory for Master's in Urban Affairs.
    Also offers Master's by course work alone.

II Not published.

III Available for library rerefence only in the
    Reference Department.
    Not available for personal loan or inter-library loan.

IV Copyright is held by the author.
    Author's permission is required for copying.
    Copies may be made available by contacting the
    author.

V   Listed in a special catalogue of theses.

VI Copies are also held in the office of the Director of
    Graduate Studies.

159 NORTH AMERICAN BAPTIST SEMINARY

Kaiser-Ramaker Library
1321 West 22. Sioux Falls. South Dakota 57105

I   Doctoral (1,3,2); Master's (2,0,2).
    Thesis is awarded 20% of total course credit for
    Doctorate and 2-6% for Master's.
    2 copies are deposited.

II Not published.

III No restrictions on library access.
    Not available for personal loan.
    Photocopy is available for inter-library loan within
    the U.S.A. only.

IV Copyright is held by the author.
    No special restrictions on copying.
    Not available for purchase or exchange.

V   Listed in the Library's catalogue and a special
    catalogue of theses.
    Listed in *American Doctoral dissertations.*
    D.Min. projects are being indexed in American
    Theological Library Associations - *Research in
    Ministry.*

VI -

160   OBLATE COLLEGE

Oblate College Library
391 Michigan Avenue N.E.
Washington, D.C. 20017

I   Master's (1,1,2).

II   Not published.

III No restrictions on library access.
Original is available for personal loan and inter-
library loan within the U.S.A. and abroad.

IV   Copyright is held by the author.
No special restrictions on copying.
Not available for exchange.

V   Listed in the Library's catalogue.

VI   -

161   OCCIDENTAL COLLEGE

Special Collections Librarian
Occidental College Library
1600 Campus Road
Los Angeles, California 90041

I   Master's (9,20,11).
Degree is by course work and thesis.

II   Not published.

III Not available for personal loan unless a second
copy exists.
Photocopy is available for inter-library loan within
the U.S.A. and abroad.

IV   Copyright is held by the author.
Permission of the author is required for copying.
Not available for exchange.

V   Listed in the Library's catalogue and a special
catalogue of theses.

VI   -

162   PEABODY COLLEGE OF VANDERBILT UNIVERSITY

Inter-Library Loan Assistant
Education Library
Nashville, Tennessee 37203-6501

I   Doctoral (45,140,173); Master's (139,348,265).
Both degrees are completed by course work and
thesis.
2 copies are deposited.

II   Not published.

III No restrictions on library access.
Available for personal loan.
Photocopy or circulating copy is available for inter-library loan if the thesis is not availiable through University Microfilms.
Postage and handling would be charged.

IV Copyright is held by the author.
No special restrictions on copying.

V Listed in the Library's catalogue and *Dissertation abstracts international.*

VI -

163 PEABODY INSTITUTE OF THE JOHNS HOPKINS UNIVERSITY

Librarian
Peabody Conservatory Library
1 East Mount, Vernon Place
Baltimore, Maryland 21202

I Doctoral (5,9,2); Master's.
Thesis is awarded 10% of total credit for Doctorate and 20% credit for Master's in Music History.
2 copies are deposited. 1 copy of composition portfolios is deposited.

II Published by University Microfilms.

III No restrictions on library access.
Not available for personal loan.
Original is available for inter-library loan within the U.S.A. and abroad.

IV Copyright is held by the author.
Author's permission is required before making complete copies.
Available for purchase with permission of the author.
Not available for exchange.

V Listed in the Library's catalogue.
Listed in *International index of dissertations and musicological works in progress* edited by C. Adkins and A. Dickinson. Philadelphia, American Musicological Society, 1977. First Supplement 1979.
Listed in *Repertoire International de Littérature Musicale* (RILM abstracts) and *Dissertation abstracts international.*

VI Theses presented since 1980 are available from University Microfilms.

164   PENNSYLVANIA COLLEGE OF PEDIATRIC MEDICINE

College Librarian
Charles E. Krausz Library
8th at Race Streets
Philadelphia, Pennsylvania 19107

I   Master's (1,2,1).
Thesis is awarded 50% of total course credit.

II   Not published.

III No restrictions on library access.
Available for personal loan.
Photocopy is available for inter-library loan within the U.S.A. and abroad.

IV   Copyright is held by the author.
Not available for exchange.

V   Listed in the Library's catalogue.

VI   -

165   PHILADELPHIA COLLEGE OF ART

Library Director
Albert M. Greenfield Library
Broad and Spruce Streets, Philadelphia
Pennsylvania 19102

I   Master's (3,4,3).
Degree is by course work and thesis.

II   One thesis has been published as a book to date.

III No restrictions on library access.
Not available for personal loan.
Availability would depend on the author's agreement.

IV   Copyright holder varies.
Author's permission is required for copying.
Some theses would be available for exchange, with catalogue cards included.

V   Listed in the Library's catalogue.

VI   Most theses are largely visual images (slides, illustrations, etc.) making copying difficult and costly.

166 PHILADELPHIA COLLEGE OF PHARMACY AND SCIENCE

Rare Book Librarian
Joseph W. England Library
42nd Street and Woodland Avenue
Philadelphia, Pennsylvania 19104

I Doctoral (5,7,1); Master's.
3 units for research thesis and 52 credits for course work for Doctorate; 26 credits for course work and 4 credits for research for Master's (no formal thesis).
2 copies of Doctoral theses are deposited.

II Published in printed format or microform.

III Bound copies are available for library reference.
Not available for personal loan.
Photocopy is available for inter-library loan within the U.S.A. and abroad.

IV Copyright is held by the author.
Photocopy is available ($4.00 per request up to 30 pages and 25 cents per page plus postage-prepaid).
Not available for purchase or exchange. Microfilm copy is available for photoreproduction at a fee.

V Listed in the Library's catalogue and the OCLC : Ohio College Library Center data base.
Listed in *Dissertation abstracts international.*

VI -

167 POINT LOMA COLLEGE

Interlibrary Loan Department
Ryan Library
3900 Lomaland Drive
San Diego, California 92106-2899

I Master's.
Thesis or project is optional. Previously theses were required.
2 copies are deposited.

II Not published.

III No restrictions on library access.
Available for personal loan and inter-library loan within the U.S.A.

IV Copyright is held by the author.
Permission is required for copying.
Not available for purchase or exchange.

V Listed in the Library's catalogue.

VI -

168 QUEEN'S COLLEGE, COLUMBIA UNIVERSITY OF NEW YORK

Director
Paul Klapper Library
65 - 30 Kissena Boulevarde, Flushing
New York 11367

I   Master's (-,-,51) 65 in 1982.
Some theses only are deposited.

II   Not published.

III   Not available for personal loan.
Photocopy is available for inter-library loan within the U.S.A.

IV   Copyright is held by the author.
Researchers must acknowledge willingness to abide by copyright covenant.
Not available for purchase or exchange.

V   Listed in the Library's catalogue.

VI   -

169 REGIS COLLEGE

Librarian
Regis Library
335 Wellesley Street, Weston
Massachusetts 02193

I   Master's (12,7,13).

II   Not published.

III   No restrictions on library access.
Available for personal loan.
Not available for inter-library loan.

IV   No special restrictions on copying.
Not available for exchange.

V   Listed in the Library's catalogue.

VI   -

170 ROCHESTER INSTITUTE OF TECHNOLOGY

Archivist
Wallace Memorial Library Archives
1 Lomb Memorial Drive
Rochester, New York 14623

I   Master's (65,87,80).
Percentage of credit for thesis varies from college to college.

II   Not published.

III Available for use in the Archives Room or at the Reference Desk only.
Author's permission is required for personal loan.
A photocopy is available for inter-library loan within the U.S.A. and abroad.

IV Copyright is held by the author.
Author's permission is required for copying.
Not available for exchange.

V Listed in the Library's catalogue.
Master's in F.A. Photography are listed in an internal bibliography.

VI Visitors are welcomed to use theses in the Archives Room during normal working hours.

171 SAINT JOSEPH COLLEGE

Library Director
Pope Pius XII Library
1678 Asylum Avenue. West Hartford
Connecticut 06117

I Master's (1,0,3).
Thesis is optional.
Also offers Master's by course work alone.

II Infrequently published by private publishing houses.

III No restrictions on library access.
Available for personal loan.
Original is available for inter-library loan within the U.S.A. and abroad.

IV Copyright is held by the author.
Copying beyond general copyright restrictions requires author's permission.
Not available for purchase or exchange.

V Listed in the library's catalogue.
Listed in *Master's theses in education* and *Master's theses in pure and applied sciences.*

VI -

172 SAINT JOSEPH'S UNIVERSITY

Drexel Library
5600 City Avenue. Philadelphia
Pennsylvania 19131

I Master's (6,4,3).
Degree is by course work and thesis and by thesis alone.

II Not published.

III No restrictions on library access.
Available for library use only.

IV Copyright is held by the institution.
Permission of the teaching department concerned
is required for copying.
Not available for exchange.

V Listed in the Library's catalogue.

VI -

173 SAINT PAUL SEMINARY

John Ireland Memorial Library
2260 Summit Avenue, St. Paul, Minnesota 55105

I Master's (27,24,21).
Thesis is awarded 10% of total course credit.

II Not published.

III Available for library reference only.
Not available for personal loan or inter-library loan.

IV Copyright is held by the author.
No special restrictions on copying.
Not available for purchase or exchange.

V Not listed in catalogues or bibliographies.

VI -

174 SARAH LAWRENCE COLLEGE

Librarian
Esther Raushenbush Library
Bronxville, New York 10708

I Master's (11,17,21).
Degree is by course work and thesis.
2 copies are deposited.

II Published by University Microfilms in printed copy
and microform.

III For library access users must sign an agreement
not to reproduce any material.
Available for personal loan.
Photocopy is available for inter-library loan within
the U.S.A.

IV Copyright is held by the author.
Copying is not permitted.
Not available for purchase or exchange.

V Listed in the Library's catalogue.
Listed in *Dissertation abstracts international* and the
OCLC : Ohio College Library Center data base.

VI -

175   SCARRITT COLLEGE FOR CHRISTIAN WORKERS

Virginia Davis Laskey Library
Nashville, Tennessee, 37203 - 4466

I   Master's (10,8,-).
Theses were required in some areas between
1925-1981.
Now are completed by course work alone.
2 copies were deposited.

II   Not published.

III   No restrictions on library access.
Photocopy is available for inter-library loan
abroad.

IV   Copyright is held by the author.
Copying is restricted to one copy of thesis per
request.
Available for exchange. Catalogue cards are not
included.

V   Listed in the Library's catalogue and a special
catalogue of theses.

VI   -

176   SCHOOL OF THEOLOGY AT CLAREMONT

Thesis Secretary
Theology Library
1325 North College, Claremont
California 91711

I   Doctoral (37,32,34).
Degree is by course work and thesis (100% of
credit).

II   Published by University Microfilms.

III   No restrictions on library access.
Not available for personal loan or inter-library loan.

IV   Copyright is held by the author.
No special restrictions on copying.
Available for purchase through University
Microfilms.

V   Listed in the Library's catalogue, a special
catalogue of theses and *Dissertation abstracts
international.*

VI   -

177 SONOMA STATE UNIVERSITY

Technical Services Office Manager
Ruben Salazar Library
1801 East Cotati Avenue, Rohnert Park
California

I   Master's (40,327,36).
Degree is by course work and thesis.
2 copies are deposited - one circulating copy and
one for Library Archives.

II Published in printed format by the author.

III Available for personal loan and inter-library loan
within the U.S.A. only.

IV Copyright is held by the institution.
Restrictions on copying any part may be made by
the author.
Not available for exchange.

V   Listed in the Library's catalogue and a special
catalogue of theses.
Listed in the OCLC : Ohio College Library Center
data base.

VI -

**178 SOUTHEASTERN BAPTIST THEOLOGICAL
SEMINARY**

Librarian
Southeastern Seminary Library
PO Box 752, Wake Forest, North Carolina 27587

I   Doctoral (12,15,10); Master's (3,11,11).
Degrees are by course work and thesis.
Also offers Master's by course work alone.
2 copies are deposited.

II Published in microform by the Historical
Commission, Southern Baptist Convention,
Nashville, Tennessee.

III No restrictions on library access.
Photocopy is available for personal loan and inter-
library loan within the U.S.A. and abroad.

IV Copyright is held by the institution.
Permission is required for copying.
Microform copies are available for purchase from
the Historical Commission, Southern Baptist
Covention.
Would consider exchange.

V   Listed in the Library's catalogue and a special
catalogue of theses.

VI -

179 SOUTHERN BAPTIST THEOLOGICAL SEMINARY

Inter-library Loans Clerk
James P. Boyce Centennial Library
2825 Lexington Road, Louisville
Kentucky 40208

I Doctoral (26,24,20); Master's (5,10,6);
Thesis is awarded 50% of credit for Doctorate.
2 copies are deposited.

II Published by University Microfilms.

III No restrictions on library access.
Not available for personal loan or inter-library loan.

IV Copyright is held by the author.
No special restrictions on copying.
Available for purchase from University Microfilms
and the Historical Commission, Southern Baptist
Convention, Nashville, Tennessee.
Not available for exchange.

V Listed in the Library's catalogue and *Dissertation
abstracts international.*

VI -

180 SOUTHERN CONNECTICUT STATE COLLEGE

Buley Library
501 Crescent Street
New Haven. Connecticut 06515

I Master's (74,34,42); Postgraduate diploma.
Thesis is one of three options except in clinical
programmes where no thesis option exists.

II Not published.

III Available for library use only with deposit of a valid
I.D. card.
Not available for personal loan.
Original is available for inter-library loan within the
U.S.A. only.
Copies can be made for foreign distribution at a
charge.

IV No copyright held.
No special restrictions on copying.
Available for purchase.

V Listed in the Library's catalogue and a special
catalogue of theses.

VI Copies are deposited with 3 other Connecticut
State Colleges (Central, Eastern and Western).

181   SPRINGFIELD COLLEGE

Reference Librarian
Babson Library
Springfield, Massachusetts 01109

I   Doctoral (3,5,5); Master's (20,12,18).
Doctorate completed by course work and theses.
Students may elect to do Master's by course work
and thesis or course work alone.
3 copies are deposited.

II   Select theses are published in microform by the
University of Oregon.

III   Archival copy for library use only on deposit of an
I.D. card.
Circulating copies are available for inter-library
loan within the U.S.A. and abroad.

IV   Copyright is held by the author.
No special restrictions on copying.
Not available for purchase or exchange.

V   Listed in the Library's catalogue.
Selected theses are listed in the microforms
publication bulletin of the University of Oregon
and in *Completed research of the AAHPERD*
(American Association for Health, Physical Education
Recreation and Dance).

VI   -

182   SWARTHMORE COLLEGE

Special Collections Librarian
McCabe Library
Swarthmore, Pennsylvania 19081

I   Master's (3,1,0).
Thesis is awarded 25% of total course credit.

II   Not published.

III   No restrictions on library access.
Available for personal loan.
Original is available for inter-library loan within the
U.S.A. and abroad.

IV   Copyright is held by the author.
No special restrictions on copying.
Not available for purchase or exchange.

V   Listed in the Library's catalogue.

VI   -

183 TRINITY COLLEGE

Trinity College Library
300 Summit Street, Hartford
Connecticut 06106

I   Master's (27,20,29).
Credit for thesis varies.

II   Not published.

III   No restrictions on library access.
Not available for personal loan or inter-library loan.

IV   Copyright is held by the author.
Author's written permission is required for copying.
Not available for purchase or exchange.

V   Listed in the Library's catalogue and a special catalogue of theses.

VI   -

184 TRINITY EVANGELICAL DIVINITY SCHOOL

Reference Librarian
Rolfing Memorial Library
2065 Half Day Road, Bannockburn
Deerfield, Illinois 60015

I   Doctoral (4,15,17); Master's (45,39,41).
Doctoral thesis is awarded 1/9th of course credit.
2 copies are deposited.

II   Not published.

III   No restrictions on library access.
Available for personal loan.
Circulating copy is available for inter-library loan within the U.S.A. Photocopy is available for loan abroad.

IV   Copyright is held by the authors if they choose.
No special restrictions on copying.
Not available for purchase or exchange.

V   Listed in the Library's catalogue and a special catalogue of theses.
Listed in *Cumulative dissertation index* and the School's published list of theses with annual updates.

VI   -

185 TRINITY LUTHERAN SEMINARY

Librarian
Library
2199E Main Street, Columbus, Ohio 43209

I Doctoral (2,3,3); Master's (3,3,2); Postgraduate diploma (73,57,65).
Thesis is awarded 50% of total credit for Doctorate and 33.3% of credit for Master's.
From 1982 onwards 2 copies of Doctoral theses are deposited.

II Not published.

III Available for library reference only with the Librarian's permission.
Not generally available for personal loan or inter-library loan.

IV Copyright is held by the author.
Permission of the Librarian is required for copying.
Not available for purchase or exchange.

V Listed in the Library's catalogue.
From 1982 Doctoral theses have been abstracted by the American Theological Library Association.

VI -

186 VASSAR COLLEGE

Curator of Rare Books and Manuscripts
Vassar College Library
Box 20, Poughkeepsie, New York 12601

I Master's (1,1,2).
Thesis is awarded 25% of total course credit.
2 copies are deposited.

II Not published though author may initiate publication.

III No restrictions on library access.
Not available for personal loan or inter-library loan.

IV Copyright is held by the author.
Author's written permission is required for copying.
Not available for purchase or exchange.

V Listed in the Library's catalogue and a special catalogue of theses.

VI -

187 VIRGINIA STATE UNIVERSITY

Inter-Library Loans
Johnston Memorial Library
PO Box JJ, Petersburg, Virginia 23803

I Master's.
Theses are not required for all programmes.
2 copies are deposited.

II   Not published.

III   No restrictions on library access.
Available for personal loan and inter-library loan within the U.S.A. and abroad.

IV   Copyright is held by the author.
Author's permission is required for copying.
Not available for purchase or exchange.

V   Listed in the Library's catalogue and a special catalogue of theses.

VI   -

188   WALLA WALLA COLLEGE

Director of Libraries
Peterson Memorial Library
College Place, Washington 99324

I   Master's (13,15,14).
Thesis is awarded 18% of total course credit.
2 copies are deposited.

II   Published in scientific journals.

III   No restrictions on library access.
Available for personal loan.
Photocopy is available for inter-library loan within the U.S.A. and abroad.

IV   May be copyrighted by the author or journal publisher.
Not available for purchase or exchange.

V   Listed in the Library's catalogue.

VI   -

189   WEBSTER COLLEGE

Library Director
Eden-Webster Libraries
475 East Lockwood Avenue
St. Louis, Missouri 63119

I   Master's.
Thesis is awarded 16.6% of total credit and is optional in many areas.

II   Not published.

III   No restrictions on library access.
Not available for personal loan.
Photocopy is available for inter-library loan within the U.S.A. and abroad.

IV   No special restrictions on copying.
Not available for purchase or exchange.

V   Listed in the Library's catalogue.

VI   -

190 WEST CHESTER UNIVERSITY

Special Collections Librarian
Francis Harvey Green Library
West Chester, Pennsylvania 19083

I   Master's (12,13,17).
Thesis is awarded 5% of total course credit.
2 copies are deposited.

II   Not published.

III   Archival copy is to be used in the Special
Collections Room only.
Circulation copy is available for loan.
Photocopy is available for inter-library loan within
the U.S.A. and abroad.

IV   Copyright is held by the author.
Permission of author is required for copying of
substantial parts.
Not available for purchase or exchange.

V   Listed in the Library's catalogue.
Listed in the OCLC : Ohio College Library Center
data base.

VI   -

191 WEST VIRGINIA COLLEGE OF GRADUATE STUDIES

Public Service Librarian
Institute, West Virginia 25064

I   Master's.
Thesis is awarded 16.6% of total course credit.

II   Not published.

III   No restrictions on library access.
Available for library reference only.

IV   Copyright is held by the author and the institution.
No special restrictions on copying.
Not available for purchase or exchange.

V   Listed in the library's catalogue and the OCLC :
Ohio College Library Center data base.

VI   -

192 WESTERN MARYLAND COLLEGE

Associate Librarian
Hoover Library
Westminster, Maryland 21157

I   Master's (0,5,1).
Thesis is awarded 15% of total course credit but is
only now required for M.Ed.
2 copies are deposited.

II   Not published.

III No restrictions on library access.
     Available for personal loan.
     Original is available for inter-library loan within the
     U.S.A. and abroad.

IV   Copyright is held by the author.
     No special restrictions on copying.
     Available for purchase.
     Not available for exchange.

V   Listed in the Library's catalogue.
     Listed in *Masters theses in education.*

VI   -

193   WESTERN THEOLOGICAL SEMINARY

John Walter Beardslee Library
Holland. Michigan 49423

I   Doctoral (0,2,2); Master's (32,26,34).
     Both are by course work and thesis.
     2 copies are deposited.

II   May be published in various forms.

III No restrictions on library access.
     Available for personal loan.
     Photocopy is available for inter-library loan within
     the U.S.A. and abroad.

IV   Copyright is held by the author.
     No special restrictions on copying.
     Available for purchase and exchange.

V   Listed in the Library's catalogue; a special
     catalogue of theses, the OCLC : Ohio College
     Library Center data base, *Dissertation abstracts
     international* and *ATLA Religion index.*

VI   -

194   WHITTIER COLLEGE

Reference Librarian
Wardman Library
Whittier. California 90608

I   Master's (2,4,5).
     Percentage of credit awarded for thesis varies by
     department - 16.6% to 25%.
     2 copies are deposited.

II   Not published.

III No restrictions on library access.
     Personal loan available to staff and students.
     Original is available for inter-library loan within the
     U.S.A.

IV   Copyright is held by the institution unless individual wishes to file for copyright.
Copyright holder's permission is required for copying.
Not available for exchange.

V   Listed in a special catalogue of theses.

VI   -

195   WHITWORTH COLLEGE

Public Service Librarian
Library
Spokane, Washington 99251

I   Master's (110,85,114).
Degree is by course work and thesis.
2 copies are deposited. Project reports are evaluated for quality.

II   Not published.

III   No restrictions on library access.
Available for personal loan.
Original is available for inter-library loan within the U.S.A. and abroad.

IV   Copyright is held by the author.
No special restrictions on copying.
Not available for purchase or exchange.

V   Listed in the Library's catalogue.

VI   -

196   WOODS HOLE OCEANOGRAPHIC INSTITUTION

Marine Biological Laboratory Library
Woods Hole, Massachusetts 02543

I   Doctoral (7,19,9); Ocean Engineer (3,1,1).
Credit for thesis varies.

II   Not published.

III   No restrictions on library access.
Available for personal loan.
Original is available for inter-library loan within the U.S.A. only.

IV   Copyright is held by the author.
No special restrictions on copying.
Available for purchase.
Not available for exchange.

V   Listed in the Library's catalogue and *Dissertation abstracts international.*

VI   Copies are deposited with the Massachusetts Institute of Technology and available from their Micro-reproduction Laboratory.

197 WORCESTER POLYTECHNIC INSTITUTE

Reference and Inter-library Loan Librarian
Gordon Library
Worcester, Massachusetts 01609

I Doctoral (5,2,8); Master's (90,103,86).
Both are by course work and thesis.
2 copies of Master's theses are deposited.

II Not published.

III Restricted access may be imposed by the
department.
Available for personal loan.
Photocopy or microform available for inter-library
loan within the U.S.A. only.

IV Copyright is held by the author.
No special restrictions on copying.
Microfilm copies of Doctoral theses are available
from University Microfilms.
Photocopies of Master's theses are available for
purchase.
Not available for exchange.

V Listed in the Library's catalogue.
Doctoral theses listed in *Dissertation abstracts
international. Americal Doctoral dissertations* and
Masters theses in the pure and applied sciences.

VI -

198 WRIGHT INSTITUTE

Librarian
Malsow Memorial Library
2728 Durant Avenue
Berkeley, California 94704

I Doctors (14, 26,21); Master's (3,10,1).
Both are by course work and thesis.
2 copies are deposited.

II Not published.

III No restrictions on library access.
Available for personal loan.
Photocopy is available for inter-library loan within
the U.S.A. and abroad.

IV Copyright is held by the author.
No special restrictions on copying.
Not available for purchase or exchange.
Available from University Microfilms.

V Listed in a special catalogue of theses.
Listed in University Microfilms - *Comprehensive
dissertations index.*

VI -

VATICAN CITY

199 PONTIFICIA UNIVERSITÀ LATERANENSE

Bibliotecario Generale
Biblioteca Generale
Piazza S. Giovanni in Laterano 4-1-00120

I Doctoral (59,40,69); Master's; Postgraduate diploma.
1 copy of unpublished and 80 copies of published Doctoral theses are deposited.

II Publishing is arranged by the author.

III Author's written permission is required for library access to unpublished theses.

IV Copyright of unpublished theses is held by the author.
Author's written permission is required for copying of unpublished theses.
Available for purchase.
Prepared to exchange published theses without catalogue cards.

VI -

Institution Index

Geographic Index

Australia:	Adelaide 8; Brisbane 6; Canberra 1; Launceston 10; Lidcombe 3; Melbourne 2,4,7,9,11; Perth 12; Sydney 15.
Canada:	Halifax 15;; Ottawa 13,17; Saskatoon 14; Toronto 16.
Chile:	Santiago 18.
Denmark:	Århus 20; Copenhagen 19,21,22.
Finland:	Helsinki 23; Kuopio 24; Vaasa 25.
France:	Lille 28; Lyon 27; Paris 26; Saint-Ouen 29.
Germany, Fed. Rep (BRD):	Clausthal 34; Flensburg 33; Hamburg 31; Hildesheim 32; Oldenburg 36; Trier 35; Tübingen 30.
India:	Madras 37.
Israel:	Rehevot 38.
Italy:	Rome 39,40,41.
Ivory Coast:	Abidjan 42.
Japan:	Osaka 43; Otaru 44; Tokyo 45.
Kenya:	Nairobi 46.
Netherlands:	Amsterdam 48; Enschede 47; The Hague 49.
Norway:	Bergen 51; Oslo 50,52,53.
Peru:	Lima 54.
Phillipines:	Dagupan City 56; Iloilo City 59; Manila 57,58; Tacloban City 55.
Poland:	Bydgoszcz 66; Cracow 61,71; Katowice 69; Kielce 68; Łódź 62; Olsztyn-Kortowo 64; Opole 70; Poznań 60,63; Wrocław 65,67.
South Africa:	Cape Town 72; Johannesburg 75; Port Elizabeth 73; Pretoria 74.
Spain:	Burgos 76; Granada 77; Vitoria 78.
Switzerland:	Lausanne 79; Luzern 80.
United Kingdom:	Aberystwyth 84; Brighton 81; Hatfield 85; Huddersfield 95; Leeds 87; Liverpool 88; London 83,86,89,90,91,96,98; Newtownabbey 99; Oxford 92; Paisley 93; Plymouth 94; Redruth 82; Sheffield 97.

United States: Alamosa 100; Albany 101; Allendale 135;
Appleton 139; Augusta 148; Bakersfield 111;
Baltimore 106,123,163; Belmont City 117;
Berkeley 134,198; Bethany 107; Boston 108,126;
Bryn Mawr 110; Butte 154; Chicago 102,138,142;
Claremont 176; Clarion 114; Cleveland 115;
Clinton 153; Columbus 185; Dallas 124; Decatur
118; Deerfield 184; Downer's Grove 131; Erie 130;
Fitchburg 127; Florence 128; Fort Wayne 120;
Glendale 103; Hartford 183; Holland 193; Hollins
College 137; Institute 191; Jackson 140; Kansas
City 113,156; Keene 143; Kutztown 144; La
Grande 125; Los Angeles 155,161; Louisville 179;
Mill Valley 133; Milwaukee 149, 152; Nashville
150,162,175; Newhaven 180; New London 121;
New York 109,122,136,141,147,157,168,174,186;
Norfolk 158; North Manchester 146; Oakland 151;
Pasadena 104,129; Petersburg 187; Philadelphia
145,164,165,166,172; Rochester 116,170; Rohnert
Park 177; St. Louis 189; St. Paul 173; San Diego
167; Seward 119; Sioux Falls 105,159; Spokane
195; Springfield 181; Statesboro 132; Swarthmore
182; Turlock 112; Wake Forest 178; Walla Walla
188; Washington 160; West Chester 190; West
Hartford 171; Westminster 192; Weston 169;
Whittier 194; Woods Hole 196; Worcester 197.

Vatican City: 199.

Numbers in brackets are those of the Dewey Decimal Classification.

Agriculture (630)   Israel 38; Netherlands 47,49; Phillipines 59; Poland 64,65,66; Switzerland 79; United States 112,139.

Architecture (720)   Australia 5,7,10; Norway 50; South Africa 73,75; Switzerland 79; United Kingdom 84,92,95; United States 110,136,157,165.

Astronomy and Surveying (520)
Australia 8,12; Israel 38; Netherlands 47; Philippines 56; Poland 65,70; United Kingdom 93; United States 110,182,190.

Biography and Genealogy (920)
United States 110,120,136,177.

Botany (580)   Australia 6,7; Finland 24; Germany, Fed.Rep.(BRD) 36; Israel 38; Netherlands 47; Philippines 56; Poland 64; United Kingdom 83,90,93,95; United States 114,121,136,139, 144,196,197.

Building (690)   Australia 5,7,10; France 27; Poland 64; South Africa 73,75; United Kingdom 84,95; United States 132,140,197.

Business and Management (650)
Australia 1,2,5,7,9,12; Denmark 20,21; Finland 23,25; Kenya 46; Norway 51; Peru 54; Philippines 56,58; Poland 60,64,70; South Africa 73,74,75; United Kingdom 84,90,93,95; United States 103,107,111,131,135,140,152,157, 170,172,194.

Chemical and Related Technologies (660)
Australia 5,6,7,8,9,12; Germany, Fed.Rep.(BRD) 36; Israel 38; Peru 54; Philippines 56; Poland 70; South Africa 73,75; Switzerland 79; United Kingdom 82,93,95; United States 139,165,197.

Chemistry and Allied Sciences (540)
Australia 2,5,6,7,8,9,11,12; Finland 24; France 27; Germany, Fed.Rep.(BRD) 36; Israel 38; Philippines 56,58; Poland 60,70; South Africa 73,74,75; Switzerland 79; United Kingdom 83,90,92,93,95; United States 110,121,139,140, 170,183,186,196,197.

Commerce (380)   Australia 7,9,10; Finland 23; Peru 54; Philippines 56; Poland 70; South Africa 73,75; United Kingdom 83,95; United States 120,158.

Communication Disorders (616.855)
Australia 3; United States 126.

Computing (001.64) Israel 38; United States 170.

Creative Writing (808) United States 126,174.

Earth Sciences (550) Australia 5,6,7,8; Germany, Fed.Rep.(BRD) 36; Israel 38; Netherlands 47; United Kingdom 82,83,90,92,93,95; United States 110,154,190, 196.

Economics (330) Australia 1,10; Denmark 20,21; Finland 23,25; Germany, Fed.Rep.(BRD) 36; Japan 44; Netherlands 49; Norway 51; Peru 54; Philippines 56; Poland 60,64,70; South Africa 73,75; United Kingdom 83,93,95; United States 110,120,140,157,183,189.

Education (370) Australia 1,2,4,10,12; Chile 18; Denmark 19; Germany, Fed.Rep.(BRD) 31,32,33,36; Israel 38; Norway 52; Philippines 56,57,58,59; Poland 64,70; South Africa 73; United Kingdom 95; United States 107,110,112,114,117,119, 120,123,125,127,131,135,136,140,144,145, 146,151,153,155,158,161,162,165,167,169, 172,175,177,181,188,189,190,192,194,195; Vatican City 199;

Engineering (620) Australia 2,5,6,8,11,12; Finland 24; France 27,28,29; Germany, Fed.Rep.(BRD) 31; Israel 38; Philippines 58; Poland 60,64,66,68,70; South Africa 72,73,74,75; Switzerland 79; United Kingdom 82,87,92,93; United States 122,130,132,139,152,154,170,183,189,196,197.

Fisheries (639) Japan 45.

Geography (910) Finland 25; Germany, Fed.Rep.(BRD) 36; United Kingdom 83,95; United States 120,136.

Health Administration (362.1)
United States 111.

History (930-990) Germany, Fed.Rep.(BRD) 36; Philippines 56; Poland 70; United Kingdom 95; United States 106,110,111,120,121,132,136,140,144,153, 172,177,183,190.

Home Economics (640) Philippines 56,59; Poland 60,64; South Africa 73,75; United Kingdom 87; United States 117.

Languages (400-490) Australia 9; Denmark 20; Germany, Fed.Rep.(BRD) 36; Japan 57; Poland 70; South Africa 73; United States 110,120,129,140,145, 158,161,169,177,186,190.

Law (340)   Denmark 20; Finland 25; Norway 51;
Philippines 56; South Africa 73; United
Kingdom 83; United States 141,142,172,183.
189,190; Vatican City 199.

Library and Information Science (020)
                         Australia 1,7,8,12; Poland 71; United Kingdom
84; United States 140.

Life Sciences (570)   Australia 2,5,6,7; Finland 24; Germany,
Fed.Rep.(BRD) 36; Israel 38; Philippines 57;
Poland 64,65; South Africa 73; United
Kingdom 83,90,92,93,95; United States
110,114,132,136,139,140,144,146,148,177,186,
188,190,194,196,197.

Literature (800-890)   Australia 12; Denmark 21; Finland 25;
Germany, Fed.Rep.(BRD) 36; Japan 43,57;
Poland 70; United Kingdom 84; United States
106,110,111,117,121,126,132,136,137,144,
146,151,153,161,177,183,190.

Manufacturing (670,680)
                         Australia 5,6,7; Finland 25; France 28,29; Peru
54; Poland 70; South Africa 73; United
Kingdom 83,84,92,93,95; United States
132,139.

Mathematics (510)   Australia 2,5,6,7,8; Finland 24,25; France
27,28,29; Germany, Fed.Rep.(BRD) 36; Israel
38; Norway 51; Philippines 56,58,59; Poland
70,71; South Africa 73; Switzerland 79; United
Kingdom 83,92,93,95; United States 110,132,
140,144,161,177,197.

Medical Sciences (610) Australia 3,6,8,11,12; Denmark 22; Israel 38;
Netherlands 48; Norway 52; Philippines 57,59;
Poland 61,62,63,64,65,67,69; South Africa
73,75; Switzerland 79; United Kingdom
82,87,92,93; United States 101,129,131,135,
136,148,149,150,164,166,177,181,183,189,190,
195,197.

Music (780)   Germany, Fed.Rep.(BRD) 36; United States
102,108,115,121,133,136,140,151,161,163,165,
175,179,190.

Optometry (617.75)   United States 138.

Palaeontology (560)   Finland 24; United Kingdom 83,90,93; United
States 196.

Philosophy (100)   Canada 17; France 26;
Germany,Fed.Rep.(BRD) 36; Italy 39,41; Ivory
Coast 42; Poland 71; United States 106,110,
120,129,136,183,184,190; Vatican City 199.

Political Science (320)   Australia 2; Chile 18; Germany, Fed.Rep.(BRD)
36; Philippines 56; United Kingdom 83,95;
United States 110,120,132,140,144,169,177,190;
Vatican City 199.

Psychology (150)   Australia 2,9; Germany, Fed.Rep. (BRD) 36;
Norway 52; Philippines 57; Poland 71; United
Kingdom 83; United States 110,111,112,120,
121,128,129,137,144,158,161,174,177,181,182,
184,198; Vatican City 199.

Public Administration (350)
Australia 1,7,12; Netherlands 49; Philippines
56; Poland 70; United Kingdom 83,84,93;
United States 111,120,132,135,140,141,158,
177,189,190.

Quaker History (289.6)
United States 182.

Recreational and Performing Arts (790)
Australia 2,3,10; Norway 52; Poland 67; South
Africa 74; United States 104,121,126,131,136,
140,151,157,161,165,174,181,186,190.

Religion (200)   Canada 13,14,16,17; France 26; Germany,
Fed.Rep.(BRD) 35,36; Italy 39,40,41;
Philippines 57; Poland 71; Spain 77,78;
Switzerland 80; United Kingdom 89; United
States 106,107,110,113,116,118,120,124,129,
131,132,133,134,145,156,159,160,167,173,176,
178,179,184,185,193,195; Vatican City 199.

Social Problems and Services (360)
Chile 18; Germany, Fed.Rep.(BRD) 36; Norway
51; Philippines 56; Poland 60; United Kingdom
83,95; United States 58,110,120,131,132,141,145,
158,172,177,181.

Social Sciences (300)   Australia 2,7,9,10; Chile 18; Finland 25;
Germany, Fed.Rep.(BRD) 31,36; Italy 39;
Norway 52; Philippines 56,58; Poland 70,71;
South Africa 73,75; United Kingdom 83,93,95;
United States 110,112,120,129,132,140,
146,177,190,195; Vatican City 199.

Town Planning (710)   Australia 10,12; Finland 25; Netherlands 49;
Norway 50; Poland 64; South Africa 73,75;
United Kingdom 92; United States
104,110,136.

Veterinary Science (636.089)
Norway 53.

Visual Arts (730-770)   Australia 7; Canada 15; South Africa 73,74,75;
United Kingdom 84; United States
100,104,110,136,140,144,153,158,165,170,190.

Women's History   United States 174.

Zoology (590)   Australia 6,7; Finland 24; Israel 38; Philippines 56; Poland 64; South Africa 73; United Kingdom 83,93,95; United States 114,121,144,196,197.

Wide range of subjects areas available:

Germany, Fed.Rep.(BRD) 30; India 37; Philippines 55; United Kingdom 81,85,86,88,94,96,97,98,99; United States 100,105,109,143,191.

International Federation of Library Associations and Institutions
Series IFLA Publications
Edited by Willem R. H. Koops

1 **Special Libraries — Worldwide.** A collection of papers prepared for the Section of Special Libraries of the International Federation of Library Associations. Edited by Günther Reichardt. 1974. 360 pages. Bound. DM 68.00, IFLA members DM 51.00. ISBN 3-7940-4421-5

2 **National Library Buildings.** Proceedings of a colloquium held in Rome, 3—6 September 1973. Edited by Anthony Thompson. 1975. 144 pages. Bound DM 28.00, IFLA members DM 21.00. ISBN 3-7940-4422-3

3 **Le Contrôle bibliographique dans les pays en developpement.** Table ronde sur le contrôle bibliographique universel dans les pays en développement, Grenoble, 22—25 août 1973. Edité par Marie-Louise Bossuat, Geneviéve Feuillebois, Monique Pelletier. 1975. 165 pages. Relié. DM 38.00, pour membres d'IFLA DM 29.00. ISBN 3-7940-4423-1

4 **National and International Library Planning.** Key papers presented at the 40th Session of the IFLA General Council, Washington, D.C. 1974. Edited by Robert Vosper and Leone I. Newkirk. 1976. 162 pages. Bound. DM 38.00, IFLA members DM 29.00. ISBN 3-7940-4424-X

5 **Reading in a Changing World.** Papers presented at the 38th Session of the IFLA General Council, Budapest, 1972. Edited by Foster E. Mohrhardt. 1976. 134 pages. Bound. DM 28.00, IFLA members DM 21.00. ISBN 3-7940-4425-8

6 **The Organization of the Library Profession.** A symposium based on contributions to the 37th Session of the IFLA General Council, Liverpool, 1971. Edited by A. H. Chaplin. 1976. 2nd edition. 132 pages. Bound. DM 28.00, IFLA members DM 21.00. ISBN 3-7940-4309-X

7 **World Directory of Administrative Libraries.** A guide of libraries serving national, state, provincial, and Länder-bodies, prepared for the Sub-Section of Administrative Libraries. Edited by Otto Simmler. 1976. 474 pages. Bound. DM 60.00, IFLA members DM 45.00. ISBN 3-7940-4427-4

8 **World Directory of Map Libraries.** Compiled by the Section of Geography and Map Libraries. Edited by John A. Wolter and David K. Carrington. New edition. 1983. Approx. 350 pages. Bound approx. DM 48.00, IFLA members approx. DM 36.00. ISBN 3-598-20374-8

9 **Standards for Public Libraries.** Prepared by the IFLA Section of Public Libraries. 1977. 2nd corrected edition, 53 pages. Bound DM 16.80, IFLA members DM 12.60. ISBN 3-7940-4429-0

10 **IFLA's First Fifty Years.** Achievement and challenge in international librarianship. Edited by Willem R. H. Koops and Joachim Wieder. 1977. 158 pages. Bound. DM 36.00, IFLA members DM 27.00. ISBN 3-7940-4430-4

11 **The International Federation of Library Associations and Institutions: A selected list of references.** Edited by Edward P. Cambio. 1977. 2nd revised and expanded edition. VI, 51 pages. DM 16.80, IFLA members DM 12.60. ISBN 3-7940-4431-2

12 **Library Service to Children: An International Survey.** Edited for the Section of Children's Libraries by Colin Ray. New edition. 1983. Approx. 158 pages. Approx. DM 36.00, IFLA members approx. DM 27.00. ISBN 3-7940-4432-0

13 **Allardyce, Alex: Letters for the International Exchange of Publications.** A guide to their composition in English, French, German, Russian, Spanish. Edited by Peter Genzel. 1978. 148 pages. Bound. DM 36.00, IFLA members DM 27.00. ISBN 3-7940-4433-9

14 **Resource Sharing of Libraries in Developing Countries.** Proceedings of the 1977 IFLA/UNESCO pre-session seminar for librarians from developing countries, Antwerp University, August 30—September 4, 1977. Edited by H. D. L. Vervliet. 1979. 286 pages. Bound. DM 36.00, IFLA members DM 27.00. ISBN 3-598-20375-6

15 **Libraries for All / Bibliothèques pour tous.** A World of Books and their Readers / Le monde du livre et de ses lecteurs. Papers presented at the IFLA 50th Anniversary World Congress, Brussels 1977. Edited by Robert Vosper and Willem R. H. Koops. 1980. 163 pages. Bound. DM 36.00, IFLA members DM 27.00. ISBN 3-598-20376-4

K · G · SAUR München · New York · London · Paris
POB 71 10 09 — D-8000 München 71 — Tel. (089) 79 89 01 — Telex 5212067 saur d

International Federation of Library Associations and Institutions
Series IFLA Publications
Edited by Willem R. H. Koops

16 **Library Service for the Blind and Physically Handicapped: An International Approach.** Key Papers presented at the IFLA Conference, Štrbské Pleso, ČSSR. 1978. Edited by Frank Kurt Cylke. 1979. 106 pages. Bound. DM 30.00, IFLA members DM 22.50. ISBN 3-598-20377-2

17 **Guide to the Availability of Theses.** Compiled by the Section of University Libraries and other General Research Libraries. Edited by D. H. Borchardt and J. D. Thawley. 1981. 443 pages. Bound. DM 68.00, IFLA members DM 51.00. ISBN 3-598-20378-0

18 **Studies on the International Exchange of Publications.** Edited by P. Genzel. 1981. 125 pages. Bound. DM 32.00, IFLA members DM 24.00. ISBN 3-598-20379-9

19 **Public Library Policy.** Proceedings of the IFLA/UNESCO pre-session Seminar, Lund, Sweden August, 20—24, 1979. Edited by K. C. Harrison. 1981. 152 pages. Bound. DM 36.00, IFLA members DM 27.00. ISBN 3-598-20380-2

20 **Library Education Programmes in Developing Countries with Special Reference to Asia.** Proceedings of the Unesco/IFLA Pre-Conference Seminar, Manila, Philippines, 15—19 August 1980. Edited by Russell Bowden. 1982. 211 pages. Bound. DM 68.00, IFLA members DM 58.00. ISBN 3-598-20387-7

21 **Françoise Hébert and Wanda Noël: Copyright and Library Materials for the Handicapped.** A study prepared for the International Federation of Library Associations and Institutions. 1982. 111 pages. Bound. DM 36.00, IFLA members DM 27.00. ISBN 3-598-20381-0

22 **Education of School Librarians for Central America and Panama: Some Alternatives.** Papers presented at the Unesco/IFLA Seminar, San José, Costa Rica, 3—8 December 1978. Edited by Sigrun Klara Hannesdóttir. 1982. IV, 122 pages. Bound. DM 36.00, IFLA members DM 27.00 ISBN 3-598-20384-5

23 **Library Service for the Blind and Physically Handicapped: An International Approach.** Vol. 2. Edited by Bruce E. Massis. 1982. 123 pages. Bound. DM 32.00, IFLA members DM 24.00. ISBN 3-598-20385-3

24 **Library Interior Layout and Design.** Proceedings of the Seminar held in Frederiksdal, Denmark, June 16—20, 1980. Edited by Rolf Fuhlrott and Michael Dewe. 1982. 135 pages. Bound. DM 64.00, IFLA members DM 48.00. ISBN 3-598-20386-1

25 Maurice B. Line and Stephen Vickers: **Universal Availability of Publications.** 1983. 139 p. Bound. DM 42.00, IFLA members DM 31.50 ISBN 3-598-20387-X

26 David Overton: **Planning the Administrative Library.** 1983. 264 p. Bound. DM 48.00, IFLA members DM 36.00 ISBN 3-598-20388-8

27 Dennis D. McDonald, Eleanor J. Rodger and Jeffrey L. Squires: **International Study of Copyright of Bibliographic Records in Machine-readable Form.** A report prepared for the International Federation of Library Associations and Institutions. 1983. 149 p. Bound. DM 42.00, IFLA members DM 31.50 ISBN 3-598-20393-4

28 **Library Work for Children and Young Adults.** Edited by Geneviève Patte. 1984. 283 p. Bound. DM 68.00, IFLA members DM 51.00 ISBN 3-598-20389-6

29 **Guide to the Availability of Theses.** II Non-University Institutions. Edited by G. G. Allen and K. Deubert. Compiled by the Section of University Libraries and other General Research Libraries. 1984. VI, 124 pages. Bound. DM 42.00, IFLA members DM 33.60. ISBN 3-598-20394-2

30 **A Guide to Developing Braille and Talking Book Services.** Edited by Leslie L. Clark in collaboration with Dina N. Bedi and John M. Gill. 1984. 108 pages. Bound. DM 42.00, IFLA members DM 33.60. ISBN 3-598-20395-0

In preparation

31 **World Directory of Map Collections.** Second Edition. Edited by John A. Wolter, Ronald E. Grimm and David K. Carrington. Compiled by the Geography and Map Libraries Sub-Section. 1984. Approx. 350 p. DM 88.00. ISBN 3-598-20374-8

K · G · SAUR München · New York · London · Paris
POB 71 10 09 — D-8000 München 71 — Tel. (089) 79 89 01 — Telex 5212067 saur d